BE THE MAN

MAN

A STORY OF HOW BECOMING VULNERABLE
BUILT A MAN WHO TAKES CARE OF
HIS FAMILY AND BUSINESS

LEE TAYLOR

Re think

First published in Great Britain in 2022
by Rethink Press (www.rethinkpress.com)

© Copyright Lee Taylor

Cover image © Shutterstock | Dziobek

To all my girls and my little boy – Aga, Annabelle, Elizabeth, Lucy and Luke – I dedicate this book to you. You all make my life complete.

Contents

Foreword

Anyone ambitious who runs multiple businesses and has a family will make mistakes. In this book, Lee talks openly about the missteps he has made over the years and how he learned to cope and better himself through coaching, ultimately becoming a coach himself.

I know the accounts in this book are true, as I first met and worked with Lee six years ago through a Mastermind group I was running. He and I have stayed in touch and watched each other's careers move forward. I know the struggles he has faced, and I have seen him overcome each one to create a great life and build a successful business.

This book is an honest account of everything he went through and the lessons he learned along the way, which will immediately resonate with many. Through reading, not only will you learn the pitfalls to avoid, you will take away valuable wisdom to help in your professional and personal life – and you'll also enjoy the read.

Far from being a typical self-help book, *Be The Man* is, rather, a true account of a life lived. The real examples within will help you to think about your own situation and experiences, and to make decisions that will guide you towards success in your business and family life.

Siam Kidd
Author of *The Crypto Book: How to invest safely in Bitcoin and other cryptocurrencies*

Introduction

This book is a true story: my story. Names have been changed to protect identities, and when you meet my coach Michelle in Chapter 4, she is actually a combination of a number of people, but everything else happened exactly as I have shared. My story tells how I became the man I wanted to be, what I learned and all the mistakes I made along the way. I have been as honest as possible so you can discover what I did to turn things around. You will see how I used my mistakes to better myself and end up winning. Then the summary you will find at the end of every chapter will remind you of what we have covered to get you thinking.

Until I wrote this book, I never truly realised how negatively my business had affected my life. As I recalled the past from my memory banks, I could feel my body tightening and a sick feeling I had once constantly lived with returned. I became emotional thinking back to how I had acted and treated people. But as my journey progressed, I found a sense of hope and finally happiness returning to me.

I have seen through my work that many couples are suffering and need help. Since working from home has become more widespread, people often now live *and* work together, which can easily lead to conflict in the home and worry about the future – I know from experience how the stress of running a business from home can devastate a relationship.

In addition, I understand what it is like to be trapped in a job with no future, every day competing in the so-called 'rat race'. But I also know how to escape from both these situations. Throughout this book, I will show you how to do the same. I will help you plan and prepare for the future and gain the knowledge to come through all your problems to succeed. I will show how I turned my life around from being totally lost to building a successful business and becoming wealthy in both financial and personal terms. You will read about how I dealt with devastation and came back stronger, finally achieving clarity on what I wanted and going from stress to success.

This is not a traditional self-help book. My personal experiences will show you how a normal guy from a poor background with little education came through knock after knock to become a success. The lessons I learned will show you what to do and what *not* to do. Change is possible for anyone, and anyone can bounce back from near financial ruin.

You can avoid the mistakes so many make in life. You can take what you learn in the pages of this book and use it to better your own life and that of your partner. By the end, you will understand what you need to do to make the crucial changes to journey from stress to success. You will be able to examine your own life and work out your way forward. My easy-to-understand and entertaining story will prepare you for success in both life and business.

The moment I was told by my careers advisor that I was basically no good, which was not the first time I had been told that (nor would it be the last), was the moment I started to build my little empire. Who do you want to prove wrong? Even if it's only your own inner critic, now's the time to take control and move towards becoming the man you and your family deserve.

1
The Rat Race

I was a small but physically strong kid, a good-looking boy with a great sense of humour and quick wit. All my time and effort went into thinking about sports and having fun. School work was boring and uninspiring; it got in the way of playing football and talking to my friends. As a result, it was with a hint of nervousness that I sat down with my careers advisor to talk through options after leaving school.

The advisor, a big man in his thirties, thumbed through my school report and let out a big sigh of disappointment.

'What do you want to do when you leave school, young man?' he asked.

'Play for Arsenal,' was my quick-fire response. What followed was a multitude of reasons why that would never happen and a sales pitch leading me down the route of an unskilled job. Not surprisingly, I left the meeting feeling quite low about my future. That man had as good as said I was a failure, and I hadn't even left school. Being told that minimum wage and no prospects was the best I could expect was not what I wanted to hear. OK, maybe I wouldn't play for Arsenal, but surely I was destined for better things in life? My grades were not expected to be great; I had been told throughout school I was a bit thick and should try harder, but I did have an ability to talk and communicate well. Surely there must be something I could use my talent for?

It was no surprise to anyone when I received my GCSE grades. The highest was a C in History and English, two subjects I enjoyed. The rest were failures. An immense sinking feeling washed over me as I read the report. Maybe my careers advisor was right after all: I'd never get a good job with these grades.

Entering the adult world

The last day at school came and went. I was no longer a boy; I was a man, and as such I was expected to get a job. My parents didn't have a great deal and needed me to find employment as soon as school ended, so I did what many young people do: I took the first job I was offered. I entered the rat race.

I didn't know at the time I was in a rat race; I thought getting a job was what I needed to do. Everything I had experienced so far in my life had taught me this. Why wouldn't I get a job? The better my grades, the better the pay would be, so I wasn't expecting much.

Using my gift of the gab, I managed to blag my way into a trainee surveyor's job based in Gants Hill, just outside of London. The firm was a small one operating all over the UK. While the salary I was offered wasn't huge, I felt like I'd achieved something for the first time in my life. My parents were proud and relieved that I'd found work and I was happy to have proved my careers advisor wrong by getting what I considered a 'proper' job.

Little did I know, this was the start of a slippery slope downhill for me.

Freedom or folly?

The months rolled on, pay cheques came and went, and I enjoyed my new life. I had money, a nice job, and for the first time, people were saying I'd done well. What I wanted, though, was freedom. Something was missing. The job was OK. It wasn't hard work and I wasn't particularly ambitious, but I felt I deserved more. When I saw people around me with better cars, clothes and lifestyles, I began to crave material things.

'I want a new car,' I told my parents. The old banger I was driving didn't quite give me the image I desired.

'Well, save up for one,' was their reply, which was not what I wanted to hear.

'How about a car loan?' I asked. After what seemed like an eternity, my parents finally gave up trying to talk me out of this idea and I convinced them to help me secure funds. A building society granted me a loan of £1,500 at a cost of £80 per month, and I had the money to buy myself a better car.

What I didn't realise was I'd just taken my next step down the slippery slope, deeper into the clutches of the rat race. Now I was not only dependent on a wage, but committed to paying back a loan. I was £80 short at the end of the month before my pay cheque had even cleared, so I needed to earn more money to keep up my standard of living.

Unfortunately, I wasn't the smartest with money. I had got into a habit of visiting my local pub most nights of the week. I'm sure you can guess what came next: a young lad with £1,500 in his pocket and plenty of girls to buy drinks for. Before I knew it, I had spent the whole loan in the boozer and had nothing more than a sore head to show for it.

I was now not only on the wrong side of debt for the first time in my life, but I had no shiny new car either. The £80 was being deducted from my account and the rat race cycle of working harder for more money to pay off debts had started. Like everyone around me, I ran as fast as I could on the hamster wheel that was my job, keeping it turning and hoping I wouldn't fall off.

Despite this setback, I was still happy. The debt was manageable and people seemed to like me at work. I did OK. As long as I had beer money and could buy nice clothes, life was good. Despite being labelled 'thick', I felt I was becoming a success, and I liked to be successful. I liked the fact people looked up to me and I wanted to continue to impress them. It made me feel good and worthwhile, so I worked harder to impress even more. I believed the more I could buy things, the more impressed people would be.

Then something happened that would drive me deeper into the rat race and make it even harder to get out.

The good life

I got a girlfriend. Of course, I'd had plenty of flings with girls before, but nothing long term. This relationship was different: this girl was someone I thought I would be with for the rest of my life.

Debbie was a lovely, kind-hearted girl from a similar upbringing to me. Her dream was to meet a nice man, get married, buy a house and have children: the sort of happily ever after played out all over the world. And who was I to disappoint her?

After dating for a few years, Debbie and I bought a house together and the rat race gathered pace. We took on a mortgage to secure the property and moved in. Life was good and we were doing everything we had been told to by society. We'd left school, got a job, saved for a deposit on a house and taken out a mortgage to buy it. Then I took out another loan to buy a lovely MGF sports car.

Once again, I felt as if I had it all. People around me saw that I had grown up, got a good job, found a serious girlfriend, bought a new house and had a shiny sports car on the drive. What they failed to realise was that I was now more dependent than ever on keeping my job, as I needed the income to pay for my lifestyle. I was on the wrong side of two debts; if I lost my job, I would lose my house, car and reputation.

Debbie and I were in trouble. We had a great life, but no financial education to build that life on. We had no idea where we were going or how to prepare for when times got hard.

At the time, we had it easy and thought it would always be so. Not once did we think about what we would do if things went wrong. We never considered educating ourselves to build more wealth outside of the rat race. We were just doing what we had been taught and thought we were doing everything right.

Having changed careers a few times, I was working in the City of London for a mortgage packager. My role was to advise mortgage brokers on the best product and help them sell it. If all went well, I got a nice commission on top of my basic salary.

Thanks to my natural communication skills, I was great at my job, but I hated it. Every day, I was up early to catch the train to London, crammed in a carriage on the busy Central Line. Then I sat at a computer in the office all day, constantly taking calls and dealing with endless boring paperwork. How I hated paperwork!

Life had become dull as I worked harder and harder to pay the bills. I still had a nice-looking life to the outside world, but I was dying inside and didn't even know it. The cycle of working long hours and travelling home on sweaty, overcrowded trains was taking its toll.

Every day was like the movie *Groundhog Day* where the main character lives the same experiences over and over. I had a reputation to keep up, though. I was successful: I had nice cars and a nice holiday every year. I was doing what I thought I was supposed to, and people looked up to me. I couldn't quit because I would lose my status, my house and cars. I wouldn't be able to afford a holiday or even go out at weekends. Getting out of the rat race was not an option.

I started to dream about a different life; I wanted more. Debbie, on the other hand, was content. She was happy: her dream was coming true. What neither of us realised at the time was that our divergent wants and needs were already affecting us negatively. For now, I had to work out how I could have more, earn more money, get a better job and go to the next level. Material things made me happy, or so I thought. I craved them more and more, wanted a bigger house and better cars, but I could not afford them. I was at the limit on credit so borrowing more wasn't an option. The only way I knew to finance the lifestyle I so badly wanted – or thought I wanted – was to get a better job.

However, there was one massive problem: I had no qualifications. My grades had been awful. I wasn't skilled in anything other than sales. I needed a better sales job, but in what? Who would pay me more money? How much harder could I work? I asked myself these questions every day, always thinking about paying the bills, borrowing more money, buying new things; never thinking about saving and investing for the future. To me, this was a waste of time as it took too long. Why save and invest and have little money to spend, when you can borrow more money to buy better things?

I was almost a full member of the rat race now. The only thing I didn't have that society demanded was a child. At least I had the sense to realise a child would have been another dependant, but only because I liked my luxuries and had grown selfish. I worked hard for what I had and didn't want a kid to take anything away from me.

A wake-up call

I carried on with my life, going through the motions. I turned up for work and tried to do as little as possible. Life had become dull and uninspiring, a constant cycle of work, home, sleep, repeat. There was a temporary escape at the weekend, and I grew to look forward to Friday evenings, but Sunday was depressing, as it meant work again the next day.

'Just get through these next five days,' I would tell myself. What a way to live, wishing the week away, but this was the life I'd created for myself.

Then at work, I overheard someone talking about a thing called regulation. I listened and learned that the mortgage industry was to become regulated. Presently, anyone could sell mortgages. Because many mortgage brokers didn't understand the industry, my job as an advisor to them was necessary.

Now, though, things were changing. If my clients didn't pass exams, they would have to stop trading. Worse still, if they did pass the exams, they would not need me anymore. For the first time in my life, I was scared. I knew that my income would drop considerably, or worse, I would lose it altogether.

I couldn't rely on employment anymore. Advising brokers to sell mortgages was coming to an end. Fear turned into panic and panic caused more fear. The dream of the high life with a great job and nice house was looking shaky. Debbie didn't earn enough money to keep us both going. What would the neighbours think if I lost my cars, or even worse, my house?

This unexpected change in legislation forced me to be creative. I took out a pen and paper and wrote down the jobs I thought I could get. I wrote to all my contacts to see who could help me. Two problems hit me immediately: firstly, my grades hadn't changed – I'd done nothing to educate myself since leaving school – and secondly, all my contacts were in the mortgage world. I had no one outside of my circle of friends and colleagues to help me. I had debt and commitments and needed a job badly.

Or did I?

While writing down a list of jobs, I'd put my brain to use. I'd created a dream list of things I wanted to do and ideas to help me achieve them, which started to make my dreams real for me. It opened my mind to possibilities and ideas to explore.

On that list, I had written: 'Start my own mortgage business'. I hadn't given it much thought at the time and had written it down flippantly, and now I was unsure if I kept looking at it because nothing else on the list was suitable. Or was it because it was the one thing that inspired me?

'Could I start my own business?' I asked myself. 'How would I do it? What would I need and how much could I earn?'

I wrote all these questions down, and then answered them. The more I wrote, the more it made sense. I knew:

- The mortgage industry well
- I would have to study to pass exams
- People who could help me
- How much the brokers I advised were earning

Most importantly, I knew I could do it. OK, not having a regular wage would be scary, but if I hit the ground running, I would be fine. I could cut back a bit on spending until the commissions started coming in. I might actually enjoy being my own boss even more than working for someone.

'What should I do?' I thought as I went to bed. Then it hit me. Regulation still hadn't come in; I could start selling mortgages right now to replace my income while I studied. And I had a contact who may be able to help. And this contact had an office near to where I lived. That would mean no more travelling on the crammed Central Line.

This could work. It could be the thing to save me.

The lists I wrote in this time of uncertainty, detailing how I could improve my lot in life, really made a difference. They gave me ideas and allowed me to be creative. If I passed my exams and made solid plans to start my own business, I could probably earn more money than I was at the moment. At this stage, just earning more money was the main driving factor for me to make a change. But that was enough.

Summary

The rat race ensnares many of us. We are taught by society to study hard and get a job. We are expected to get married, buy a house and have children. This cycle often leaves us depending on a wage to support our lifestyle. Things like mortgages and car loans need paying back, taking money away from the things we really want to do. We then need to work harder to pay back what we owe.

Bearing in mind the story I have shared in this chapter, how I became ensnared by the rat race without even knowing it, take a look at your own life. Are you too on that hamster wheel, endlessly running to keep up with the Joneses? Here are a few questions to help you get some clarity on where you are now:

- Are you taking on debt to buy things you don't really need or to impress other people? (Be honest with yourself.)

- What is your motivation when you buy something on credit?

- Do you really need what you intend to buy, and if you do, are there cheaper options?

- What can you do to improve your financial education?

- What can you learn about money and how to create more of it outside of a job?

- Where do you want your life to go?

- What do you want to achieve in life?

- How will you achieve what you want?

You may not have all the answers at this stage, but don't worry. Just taking time to consider the future and list what you want is a great exercise. Writing it down on paper will make you think. I really wish I had done this years ago.

Spending time thinking about debt, how you can improve your financial education and what you want from life is essential before you move on. Having a plan in these areas of your life will help you succeed.

2
A Leap Of Faith

Goldhill Way was a small mortgage brokerage based in Essex, near to where I lived, and owned by Frank. He was one of the few of my customers who actually understood the mortgage market, so much so that I would often wonder why he used a mortgage advisor at all. Frank and I had built up a good relationship over the years, so I guess it was more about carrying on our friendship than advice.

Frank was a big man who loved nothing more than to puff on a fat cigar and drink ale in the local pub. His voice was booming, his words well spoken, and he used this combination to wow his clients. The man was knowledgeable about finance; he had forgotten more than most people will ever know on the subject, and he could definitely help me with my plans to start a mortgage business.

My mentor

I saw Frank as my mentor. He knew the business better than anyone else in my circle of acquaintances and I wanted to work alongside him. If I could talk him into letting me work freelance within his existing company, I would then be in a nice position to learn and earn with little or no outlay.

As I sat in front of Frank, I was nervous, but confident. The nerves came from my fear of quitting full-time work, departing the rat race for the first time and starting a business. The confidence was all down to Frank. To me, he was the person who would help me become a success.

'What brings you here today?' Frank bellowed jovially.

'I'm here to make you an offer you can't refuse,' I replied. Frank folded his arms and sat back, his expression suggesting he was anticipating yet another sales pitch and wondering how much money I was after. 'I want to work here,' I blurted out. 'I know regulation is coming and I see it as an end to my job, so I want to sell mortgages on a freelance basis. I'll be self-employed and split my commission with you 60/40. In return, I'll need your help to get me through the exams.'

Frank relaxed into his luxury leather office chair and let out a little smile. 'I've always respected your advice and liked your manner as a salesman, so I know you have potential,' he said with a hint of excitement. 'OK, you're in. I will train you and we can split the commission 60/40. You can have the desk over there. There is one condition, though: you advise no one until you are qualified. Until then, I will sit in on all your calls to make sure my clients get the best advice possible. When you are qualified and trained, you can advise as many clients as you wish.'

'Deal! When can I start?'

'Right now,' was the answer. 'Sit over there and I'll show you how the phone works, then I'll introduce you to the others.'

I walked to my new desk. Just like that, I had created an opportunity from an idea I'd written down a few days ago. I had the chance to work in an established office on a self-employed basis and learn from an expert. It all seemed too easy.

'How will it work?' I asked myself. 'What will happen if I don't sell?' I would need to give my boss notice that I was leaving and tell Debbie I may have no income for a while, but the negative thoughts flew away as Frank, with his unwavering positivity, bellowed out to the other brokers within the office to come and meet 'the new guy'.

New beginnings

The other brokers in the office, Mick and Ben, approached my desk and shook my hand. Both men were in their forties and seemed friendly enough.

Frank stood behind me and put both hands on my shoulders. 'Gentlemen, this is Lee, and he will be working here,' he announced. 'Lee will be learning the ropes and I will be teaching him. I bet he will soon be selling more than you two put together. Who wants to make a wager?'

Both Mick and Ben stayed silent, backing off while muttering good luck messages in my direction. As I sat, I started to feel more confident.

Frank believes in me, I thought.

A month passed and I had worked my notice with my employer. I was ready to start officially in my new role as a freelance mortgage broker, working with Frank. When I arrived at the office, I was greeted by Mick and Ben.

'Where's Frank?' I asked.

'You won't see him until midday, he only works a few hours a day,' Ben replied.

That's strange, I thought. *How can someone as successful as Frank only work a few hours a day?* This was totally against what I'd always believed.

'If you want to be a success,' society had told me, 'you need to work as hard as you can for as long as you can.' This was not a good start at all. What was I supposed to do while Frank wasn't there? He had made it quite clear that I was not to sell *anything* without his guidance.

'What are you guys doing today?' I asked.

'We have some appointments booked later on, which will hopefully lead to some sales,' Ben replied. He was clearly the talker of the two; Mick seemed nice but reserved. I could feel him studying me, but he kept his thoughts to himself, while Ben was an open book with a lot to say.

Ben will be a good source of information, I thought. *When Frank isn't here, I'll pick his brains.*

Around midday, Frank boomed into the office. He liked to make an entrance and command the attention of others.

'Good morning,' he said, tongue in cheek. 'Lee, your first lesson starts now. I like coffee and I like it black.'

Taking the hint, I proceeded to the small kitchen to make Frank's coffee. On returning to the main office, I saw him working away. The man looked focused; he had an air of authority and confidence. After placing the coffee on Frank's desk, I returned to mine. Frank never took his gaze from his computer. He worked as I waited in silence.

'Yes!' shouted Frank all of a sudden, looking in my direction. 'I just got a deal accepted, a nice little earner for me.'

The dynamics in the office are strange, I thought. *Mick and Ben arrive early and tell me they stay late, while Frank walks in at midday and only stays a few hours. But it's Frank who is laser focused and makes the money. There is a lesson here, but I'm not sure what it is.*

A few hours passed, and then Frank announced he was off.

'Where has he gone'? I asked.

'Who knows?' Ben replied, laughing. 'Frank does what he wants when he wants. If you want to learn in this business, you need to teach yourself.'

Work smarter, not harder

As I looked down at my desk, I felt lost. How would I teach myself? What should I do and where to start? A wave of anger and panic came over me. Teaching myself would mean it would take me longer to pass my exams, and I needed to earn money *now*.

No, I thought. *I made a deal with Frank to teach me. This is not on.*

As I dialled Frank's number, I ran a few sentences through my head to see how they sounded. I didn't want to come across as pushy or do anything to upset him, so I decided to keep calm and ask when the training would start.

'Your training has started,' Frank bellowed down the phone. 'You're in sales, young man, and no one is paying you unless you sell. You do not have the luxury of a basic salary anymore.'

'I know, but you said you would train me to sell. I made you coffee, watched you work, and then you left. That's hardly the training I want.'

'Look around you, Lee. What do you see?'

'Ben and Mick.'

'I bet they are talking to each other.' Frank was correct: Mick and Ben were always talking to each other. 'If you were earning no money, what would you do, Lee? Would you sit around all day chatting?'

'No, I'd do something.'

'What?' asked Frank. 'What would you do?'

I thought about this, then replied, 'I'd get a job.'

'Wrong answer! That's the easy option, your comfort zone, little baby returning to Mummy to be spoon fed. Think bigger!'

Once again, I thought hard. 'If I couldn't get a job, I'd ask for help,' I replied.

'Exactly,' said Frank. 'The first rule of sales is to ask. If you don't ask for help, no one helps you. If you don't ask for the sale, it won't magically appear. You must ask. I'm always asking, which is how I can work far fewer hours and earn way more than anyone else in my company. Always be asking for help, Lee. It's a strength. The more you ask, the more you'll learn and the better off you'll be.'

'OK, I'm asking you to help me tomorrow,' I said.

'Sure,' replied Frank. 'I'll be there at midday, so be ready.'

I'd learned a valuable lesson on my first day. I could be shy and work things out for myself, or I could be bold and ask for help, find someone like Frank to show me. If Frank helped me to be a success, I might even end up selling more than he did.

Learn and earn

Over the course of the next few months, Frank worked hard to show me how a mortgage practice operates. He educated me on what I needed to pass my exams while I put in the hard work and studied. Frank also let me practise on clients, all the while supervised by his expert eye.

This experience was different from the training I'd received as an employee; Frank's training taught me about running a small business as well. I learned essentials such as how to get clients and keep track of my accounts. With the right effort focused in the right areas, I could do very well for myself. And I liked that idea.

By the time my exams came around, I'd made some successful sales under Frank's supervision and was waiting for them to complete. If I passed the exams, I would take a massive step towards being able to sell unsupervised and help even more clients.

As it turned out, I passed my exams without any trouble and could not wait to tell Frank. I called him on the way home and shouted my news.

'Good man! I knew you would do it. Now rush back to the office – I have some news for you, too.'

As I entered the office, Frank had a big smile on his face. 'Guess what?' he asked. 'I have your first commission. The Smith case completed and I have a cheque for £1,000 with your name on it.'

Taking the cheque and sitting down, I stared at my first ever self-employed commission. A grand was a lot of money in those days, and I knew then that if I sold as a freelancer, I would earn way more than I had as an employee. I now had the qualifications I needed and was ready. Everything was going great.

But something wasn't right. Taking out a calculator, I worked out the figures.

'Frank, we agreed a 60/40 split,' I called out.

'Correct,' said Frank, '60% for me, 40% for you. What's the problem?'

'No, I meant I would get the 60%.'

'Did you ask for the 60%? Did you make the deal clear to all parties?' Frank replied.

'No, I just presumed that if I sold, I would get the bigger share.'

'So how did presuming work for you, Lee?' asked Frank. 'Not very well. Never presume anything in business. Always make sure everyone knows what's in it for them. That way, there are no nasty surprises and everyone leaves the deal happy.'

Frank went on to explain that while I was using his knowledge, office and utilities, he wouldn't have agreed to take less than 60%, and I started to feel a bit better. I'd learned three things crucial to running a successful business: I must ask for help, I must ask for the sale and I must never presume anything. I was certainly getting the education I'd hoped for. Now I needed to find out how to take my £1,000 commission and turn it into £10,000. In the past, I would have worked harder, but over the months, I had witnessed Frank working very little and making more money than anyone else in the office. How could I do that? That would be a lesson for another day; right now, I wanted to enjoy my success.

That evening, Debbie and I went out for dinner.

'What have you learned so far?' Debbie asked as she poured us both a glass of good wine. Feeling happy and relaxed, a cheque for £1,000 clearing in my bank account, I told her the three key points I had taken on board and how crucial they would be to my future success.

'Frank says I need to make sure all my clients are happy and know what to expect from the sale, then they feel like the sale is a win for them. And when I make people feel like winners, they will recommend me, and my sales will go up. I feel so good about this opportunity, Debbie. For the first time in my life, I feel in control of my own destiny. I have a choice over how my life goes. I can see a way out of the rat race. With Frank mentoring me, I will be free and happy. We will do well financially and have everything we dreamed of. All I need to do is copy him.'

Debbie took a sip of her wine, and then said, 'Will Frank let you copy him? Surely he won't want you knowing everything. What if you become more successful than he is and leave him behind?'

I thought for a while. 'I've noticed something about Frank,' I replied. 'He is successful and he talks to successful people. Frank and his friends share stories and help each other. They want each other to do well because it strengthens their group. If I can get into their group, they will all teach me.

'I read somewhere we become the product of the people we hang around with. If I hang around with Frank and his friends, I'll become successful like them. It's a simple choice: I could sit and gossip all day, or get out of my comfort zone, mix with people who know more than me, learn and earn more than either of us ever dreamed of. Which should I choose, Debbie?'

'Learn and earn,' she said with a smile. Then we raised our glasses and toasted the good life.

Summary

When I first took the courageous step to leave the rat race, I naively thought Frank would hold my hand and tell me what to do every step of the way. Instead, he allowed me to make mistakes, and then he guided me along the right path to take. This way, the learnings were so much more impactful: once I knew the price of failure, I would ensure that I never made that mistake again.

In this chapter, I've shared some of the fundamentals that are crucial to running a successful business in *any* industry. Here's a quick recap:

- Always ask if you don't know something. No question is ever stupid if you do not know the answer. Whenever I've asked questions, I've learned from the experts, and the more I learned, the more my confidence grew.

- When you want to grow and improve, look for the right people to learn from – people who are doing well – and model yourself on them. Success leaves clues and successful people will show you how to succeed. All you need to do is find them.

- Never presume anything. To get what you want in life, make sure you have agreements that are clear to everyone involved, preferably in writing so you can revisit and check the details. Written agreements give clarity and avoid arguments/ disappointment.

- Work smarter, not harder. A few hours of focus will benefit you far more than drifting aimlessly from dawn until dusk.

- Make sure you leave your clients happy. Let them know that the sale will make them a winner, because who doesn't enjoy winning? Happy clients become advocates, and word-of-mouth recommendations are invaluable for any business.

- Be sure to ask for the sale. No deal you are making in business will happen on its own.

I'd passed my exams, my first commission cheque was in the bank, I was learning from the expert and the future was bright. What happened next? Let's find out.

3
Small Steps Towards Success

Six months had passed and I was on fire. I'd taken to selling mortgages like a duck to water. These days, Frank was in the office less and less. He had become accustomed to living off my success and pulled back from the business, which sometimes made me resentful. I was putting in the hard work to keep the place running while giving up 60% of my commission; I would have to re-negotiate with Frank.

During these six months, I had come a long way. As Frank wasn't around as much, I could no longer use him as a mentor, so I invested in some courses and books on the subject of sales. By educating myself and trying new things, I improved every day.

I'd read that small positive changes over a long period of time would add up and compound into something big. At this stage, I didn't really understand what compounding was. All I knew was that I didn't need to make massive changes all at once to get a result; far better to continue to make small changes and keep practising. As long as I was consistent and didn't give up, I would get better and better at my job, and I quickly saw the benefits.

Before long, I had become the highest selling broker in the firm, even more so than Frank who took 100% of his own commission. I had made a commitment to become a pro as professionals always earn more than amateurs. Learning had certainly increased my earning potential; my commission had increased from that initial £1,000 to at least £10,000 per month. I was going places and getting noticed.

A lightbulb moment

On a wet and windy December's morning, I realised someone was missing from the office.

'Where's Mick?' I asked Ben.

'Sick,' replied Ben, looking a little lost without his sidekick. 'What are you working on today?'

I thumbed through my paperwork. 'I have three new clients lined up and I need to chase these deals to get them through,' I explained with a note of tiredness in my voice.

'You OK?' asked Ben.

'Yeah, I'm fine. I've just been working hard over the last six months. I've done a lot of deals, and although the money is good, I may have to slow down a bit.'

Ben muttered something about there only being so many hours in the day as he walked slowly to his desk. As he left, I pondered over what he had just said. When I was an employee, I'd worked hard for long hours in the rat race. Now I was self-employed, I seemed to have rejoined the same race. Frank, on the other hand, was never at work, yet he was doing well.

Then it hit me. The compounding effect of the small positive changes I was making each day was helping Frank more than me. Frank had spent many years training as a mortgage broker and an independent financial advisor (IFA). He had also spent years building a great network of clients who knew and trusted him. These clients were loyal to Frank as he gave them a great service. Then he could do something else, something much better. Frank had built a business where others worked and he could take 60% of the proceeds.

Ben was right, there were only so many hours in a day: twenty-four to be precise. Frank worked three hours a day, but his earnings were equivalent to fifty-three – his three hours, plus those of the brokers across all his businesses, which totalled at least fifty every day. I was constantly working nine to ten hours a day and making £10K per month, while Frank was working three hours a day and making far more. He didn't even have to work at all as he leveraged other people's time, so who was the winner here? Frank, of course.

Ben hadn't realised it, but he had just taught me my biggest lesson so far.

Become a success, become a mentor

'Hey, Ben,' I called across the office, 'how come you are not selling as much as others? You have been here the longest and it doesn't seem to work for you.'

Ben shot up and hurried towards me, looking relieved that someone was actually taking an interest in him.

'I don't know,' he said. 'I try my best and often get clients in front of me, but they take the information I give them and leave. Then I never hear from them again. What am I doing wrong?'

I thought for a while. 'Let's focus first on what you do well,' I said. 'Then we can figure out what we can add to make it better.' Ben clearly liked this approach as he was eager to reply.

'I'm good at talking to people,' he said. 'I quickly build trust and I'm deeply knowledgeable about the mortgage market. I've never had trouble getting people to come to the office, but they almost always leave after I have explained the details of the deal. You don't have any trouble closing, Lee, so how do you do it?'

'I kiss all my clients and they sign up with me.'

Ben roared with laughter. 'Even the men?' he asked.

'All of them,' I replied with a grin. 'I'm not sexist.'

'But seriously, how do you do it?' Ben asked, getting the conversation back on track.

'Kiss is an acronym,' I explained. 'It stands for keep it simple, Stupid. In other words, I give my clients what they need, not what I think they need. Let me explain.

'Ben, you give your clients every last detail of the deal, right?' When he agreed, I added, 'Whether they want the information or not. Let's say I am your client. I'm fairly clued up about the mortgage market and I'm a busy person who only really wants to know two things: will the lender lend to me and how much will it cost me? How would I feel if you were to sit me down for a couple of hours and explain the ins and outs of the entire mortgage market?'

'Frustrated,' said Ben.

'Exactly. And will a frustrated person buy from you?'

'Probably not,' Ben whispered.

'I would wager that the clients you sign up are the ones who want the details, the ones who thrive on your wonderful knowledge. The ones who disappear weren't given what they wanted. You didn't satisfy their needs.'

'I frustrated them,' said Ben.

'I think you may be right,' I said gently. 'You don't do anything fundamentally wrong, you just need to keep it simple until you work out if your client needs more information or not. If they don't, then why complicate things? As long as your client fully understands the deal and is happy to proceed, there is no reason to keep pushing more information their way. Find their problem and solve it, that's all you need to do.

'Everyone who comes in here has a problem they need solving. Say they want to buy a house. The problem is they don't have the cash to buy it. A mortgage solves the problem. The problem may be their house is too small, but they don't want to move. A solution could be to release equity from their home to extend, or they may prefer to take out a second mortgage. Give them the most suitable solution and you both win.

'You need to focus on their problem, find a way to fix it and explain it in easy-to-understand terms. The financial market is full of jargon that people don't understand. Take away the complication and you will see more sales.

'All of what I have told you will create more trust between you and your clients. They will see you as a problem solver and they will recommend you.'

Ben stood with a new air of purpose. 'I'll have fun kissing my clients, but I won't tell the wife,' he said with a chuckle as he walked away.

I was pleased with myself. By now I had learned a lot and was happy to teach Ben. Becoming a mentor actually did us both a lot of good: from that day, Ben started to close more and more sales, and I had reaffirmed what I knew.

Onwards and upwards

Being a successful mentor was all very well, but I wanted out of the rat race. I wanted to be like Frank. If I could only figure out how to start my own practice, then I could get people to work for me. Or maybe Frank would make me a partner if I added value to his business.

As I sat back in my living room chair after a hard day's work, I remembered that success leaves clues and the best way to be successful is to model myself on successful people. Frank had been there, seen it and done it. I could study the clues he'd left and model myself on him, and if I could emulate Frank, he would be more likely to make me a partner.

Remembering the first lesson Frank taught me, always ask, I called him straight away.

'Frank, it's Lee,' I blurted out.

'Why are you calling me so late?' he growled.

'I want to study to be an IFA just like you. I want to be more successful and make us both even more money. Will you train me?'

Frank was impressed. Not only had I become his top-selling broker, but I was hungry for more. I was going places and Frank clearly liked where I was heading.

'Sure, I'll train you. Now leave me alone to enjoy my evening.'

Frank hung up, leaving me full of excitement and wonder about the future. When Debbie walked into the room, she found me grinning like the Cheshire

Cat. It had been a while since she had seen me looking anything other than tired.

'You look happy,' she commented.

'I'm going to be an IFA,' I replied, but before I could elaborate, Debbie cut in.

'When will enough be enough, Lee? You work hard, earn good money and are always tired. We have a nice house, a nice car and lovely holidays; why do we need more? Why do you want to take on more?'

'I need to take on more so I can end up doing less,' I explained. 'I want to be like Frank. He has loads of spare time. I'm so close to making it big, Debbie, I can feel it.'

'What about kids?' Debbie asked. 'When are we going to have kids? I've been meaning to talk to you about starting a family for a while – what do you think?'

I froze with fear. She'd said the K word.

'You know I've never wanted kids,' I replied. 'You knew this when we got together.'

'We got together years ago; I was hoping you would change your mind,' Debbie said sadly.

'This house is too small for kids. Why don't we buy a bigger one in a few years and talk about it then?' I had always been a sucker for a sad face and hated seeing Debbie looking so dejected.

As it happened, Debbie and I found our dream home quickly – more quickly than I might have wanted. It was a large detached house that needed a bit of TLC, but we loved it all the same. It was everything I had ever dreamed of: four large bedrooms, three reception rooms, another room I could convert into a gym, and a large garage. It certainly was a house to be envied and I wanted people to envy me. I liked the fact it was bigger than my friends' houses. I wasn't just buying a home; I was buying a status symbol.

It was a sunny day when Debbie and I moved into our new home. As we welcomed people into our spacious rooms, I watched my guests' faces light up at the size of the property. For the first time in my life, I started to feel like I had made it.

The reality was that I was far from making it. I had got carried away by my short-term success and was in way over my head. There was trouble coming our way, and it would have a disastrous effect.

Summary

Life was looking good for me. I was earning loads of money and I was learning all the time, investing in my education to make sure I continued to improve. That all sounds great, doesn't it? Until I realised that the real winner was Frank. I was getting home exhausted every day, while he continued to scoop 60% of my earnings and only work a couple of hours a day.

It seemed I had traded one rat race for another, but things weren't all bad. The learning I was doing at this time taught me things that have been invaluable to me ever since, and believe me, they will work for you too:

- If you want to improve yourself, start small and build up. Consistently making a small improvement each day is far easier to manage than making one massive change. Small steps compound over time to make massive positive changes.

- The best investment you can make is your education. Take time to learn what you need to progress.

- Focus on what you are good at and do more of it.

- Find other people to do what you are not good at. Leverage other people's skills and time to enable you to achieve and earn more.

- Kiss your clients! Keep it simple; don't overcomplicate things just to impress them, because it won't. The more easily they can understand what you're selling, the better.

I was earning good money, living in my dream house and was the envy of all my friends. Surely nothing could go wrong.

Oh yes it could!

4
Crash!

Debbie was overjoyed when she found out she was pregnant, having finally worn me down and got my agreement to start a family. I have to admit that when it came down to it, I was chuffed with the idea of being a dad. Life was good. I was earning enough money, so losing Debbie's income wouldn't be a problem.

At this stage of life, I still evaluated everything in terms of how much I could earn and spend. Debbie wasn't a huge earner anyway, so I calculated that if I made one more sale a month, we wouldn't lose out financially if she gave up work to look after our baby. The child would keep her occupied and I'd be able to spend more time at the office, so we went for it.

Baby Annabelle was born on 11 May 2008. Debbie and I didn't know it then, but our daughter entered a world that was changing forever.

It's all over

As I walked through the doors into work later that year, I was greeted by a ranting and raving Frank. I'd never seen him so agitated.

It was 15 September 2008, a day I and many more like me would never forget.

'It's all over,' shouted Frank. 'The world is doomed; we are doomed. This collapse will end it all.'

'What are you talking about, Frank?' I asked.

'Lehman Brothers!' Frank shouted. 'Haven't you heard?' Then he paced up and down the office. I looked over at Mick and Ben, who were quiet and dejected.

'Heard what?' I asked.

'Lehman Brothers. You know who they are, don't you, Lee?'

'Of course I do,' I replied excitedly. 'I was at their Docklands premises last week; it's beautiful. I have a potential client there – you want to see his office, Frank; it's amazing.'

'Not anymore, Lee. Lehman Brothers filed for bankruptcy in the early hours of this morning.' Falling silent, Frank slumped into his big leather chair and an air of sadness descended over the entire office.

'I'll be honest with you all,' said Frank after brooding for a while, 'this is massive. You know I've been saying for ages that the subprime mortgage market is too big. There is too much exposure and now banks are going bust because of it. Please don't take this news lightly, gentlemen. I fear your incomes are going to reduce drastically very quickly.'

Over the years, I'd splashed the cash. Now earning on average £10,000 per month, I was having a lot of fun. I had just bought two new cars as well as my dream house, had a huge mortgage and was accustomed to living the high life. Money burned a hole in my pocket. Now my income was in danger of disappearing.

Commission came in from the deals that had completed, I managed to source a few new deals, and for a while, things looked OK. However, the banks were becoming increasingly unwilling to lend now. Clients were nowhere near as easy to come by as they had once been, so I found myself with spare time on my hands, which I wasn't used to.

I used this time wisely, studying for my IFA qualifications. If I passed my exams, I was sure I would be OK. I could sell investments and build my business back up.

Nowhere to turn

I reached out to my old network from my mortgage packaging days. Many of the brokers had made a switch to property, buying and selling and doing well. Some used me to source their mortgages, and some I hadn't spoken to for a long while.

Peter was one of the guys I had a good relationship with. He was a similar age to me and had premises near to Frank's. As I walked into his once buzzing office, I was greeted by a broken man.

'It's over, mate,' he yelled. 'I can't get any money. I've got houses I can't sell and I can't buy any more.'

Peter had built a nice business buying and selling houses. Like me, he enjoyed nice things: he had a big house and an M3 BMW, and loved to party on fine champagne. Splashing the cash was his way of life.

Today was different, though. Instead of telling me how much money he had, he was telling me how much he *didn't* have.

Peter and I spent an hour chatting over what he was going to do. He planned to rent all his houses out and close his office. If he cut back on the spending, he might be able to use the rent money to pay his mortgage. If he needed extra money, he would get a job, but didn't know what he could do. Property was the only thing he knew.

As I left Peter's office, I started to panic. Everyone I had spoken to was suffering. Some tried to put a brave face on things and tell me it would be OK, the market would bounce back and they would hang in there, waiting for the good times. Others like Peter were more realistic. But at least he had a plan. I had nothing; I was putting my head in the sand and hoping everything would be OK.

Over my short period of time with Frank, I'd done well and built a lovely life with lovely things. I didn't want to accept it was over and give up. This would mean failure. What would the neighbours think?

A different perspective

Of course, what I viewed as failure did eventually come. As interest rates plummeted, things got worse and worse. I had advised most clients to take out a base-rate tracker mortgage with intelligent finance. This meant they were all saving so much money as rates tumbled, not only were there no new leads coming in, but no one wanted to remortgage their current deal as they were on such a good rate.

I now had to make a choice: carry on and get my IFA exams, or quit and do something else. After talking things through with Debbie, I decided to quit. The economy was in a full recession and starting over as a newly qualified IFA didn't seem like a wise choice. The dream was over for now.

I had little in the way of savings and a big house, but as luck would have it, I also had a base-rate tracker mortgage and my payments had come down. Debbie had returned to work on a part-time basis so there was a little income to help.

It was a weird feeling, waking up each day and having nowhere to go. As I lay in bed and wondered what to do with my day, I decided a good idea would be a workout and sauna at the gym to get myself going.

The gym was full of middle-aged and older men and women. Everyone looked good and happy to be there; they seemed like they had money and a relaxed lifestyle. I thought how different the gym's atmosphere was at that time of day; I was used to the hustle and bustle of the younger crowd who worked out in the evenings and were always in a rush.

After my workout, I sat in the sauna and chatted with an attractive elderly woman.

'I've not seen you here before,' she said.

'No,' I replied. 'I usually come after work, but I just quit so thought I'd come earlier.'

'Are you wealthy?' she asked sharply. I was taken aback by her abruptness and felt slightly embarrassed.

'No,' I said. 'I had a good business selling mortgages, but it's over now. I lost my income, and to be honest, I'm worried I will lose everything.'

I started to relax as I got things off my chest. Oddly, talking to a stranger who knew nothing about me was calming. She seemed interested and listened intently.

'My girlfriend and I have just had a baby,' I went on to explain, 'so I'm worried that I won't be able to support my family. I can't sleep and I'm always on edge. I've gone from earning 10K a month to nothing. It's not fair – I did nothing wrong and don't deserve this.'

'What do you deserve?' she asked.

'I deserve to have a good business. I work hard and should be able to earn money for my family.'

The lady looked at me thoughtfully. 'You should or could earn money?' she asked.

'Both,' I said. 'I know I can because I've been earning well in the past. What's the difference anyway?'

'You say "should" like you are entitled to a salary no matter what,' she replied. 'No one is entitled to anything for nothing, so I am more interested in "could". What could you do to make more money?'

'I don't know,' I said. 'All I know is mortgages and that business has gone now. I'm stuck.' I looked down at the ground, feeling lost and dejected.

The lady raised her voice as if to wake me from my self-pity, saying something I will never forget.

'Is that true, young man? Is it true you only know about mortgages and nothing else?'

'No, it isn't,' I said. 'I also know how to sell things and I'm good at it. I know how to run a small business. I'm not great, but I know the basics and I know how to treat people. I'm really good at building relationships.'

'You're a good communicator, a good salesman and you have some business skills,' the lady repeated. 'What could you do with those skills?'

My heart rate picked up as I felt a wave of excitement come over me. This lady was right: I did know more than mortgages. Mortgages were just a product I understood; the real skill was in everything else I did.

'I see what you mean,' I said. 'I have skills and can use them to start a new business, something completely different from mortgages.'

The lady smiled widely and looked me right in the eye. 'You are what you think you are,' she said. 'If you think you are an ex-mortgage broker, that's what you will be. If you think you are something else, that's what you can become.'

'But if I want to play for Arsenal, I can't make that happen. I'm too old now,' I replied with a hint of humour.

'No, you can't,' she said. 'What you think you are has to be realistic, otherwise you won't make it happen. Decide on something you can achieve, then you will achieve something that is realistic. Why not get fit and play for another football team? It may not be Arsenal, but you will have fun all the same.'

I looked at the lady in disbelief. How did she get to be so wise? She had such a calm manner and had been able to open me up to thinking about what I could do rather than what I couldn't. Talking to her had been enlightening and I didn't want the conversation to end.

The lady rose from her seat. 'Young man,' she said, 'I've been here too long and I'm late for my meeting. It's been nice talking to you. Before I leave, may I suggest one thing?'

'Of course.'

'Go home and take out a pen and paper. Write down all the things you are good at and all the things you're not good at. Then write a list of all the things your skills could enable you to do. Within that list may be something that takes a little of what you're not good at and a lot of what you are. You may find your answer there.'

'Wow, I will surely do that,' I said. 'Thank you – I love what you did there. You worked out what I should be doing.'

'No, young man, you worked out what you *could* do. I just asked the questions.'

'What is your name?' I asked.

'Michelle,' she replied. 'I'm here most mornings. It was nice chatting to you.'

As this elegant lady left the sauna, I couldn't help noticing her air of confidence and grace. She walked across the pool area and disappeared into the changing rooms.

A new take on a familiar idea

Later that day, I took out a pen and paper and drew a line down the middle. On the left, I wrote what I'm good at, and on the right, I wrote what I don't like doing. I couldn't bring myself to write what I'm no good at.

As I filled the page, something happened inside me. I realised I was good at so many things; I had plenty of skills I could use. Excited about the possibilities ahead, I gained a renewed sense of confidence.

I then got another piece of paper and started on a list of all the things I could do to make a living. This one was a bit trickier as all I could think about were mortgages and finance, and some doubts started to creep back. I remembered my grades and how unqualified I was. Yes, I'd passed mortgage and finance exams, but what good were they now?

I knew one thing for sure: I didn't want a job. I remembered Frank telling me to think bigger when I'd stated that I would get a job if I wasn't earning money. Frank had run a business that gave him freedom. I wanted the same.

I wrote the words 'Start my own business where people work for me and I become free' in capital letters at the top of the page, and then sat back to think. What business? What would I need? How would I do it? When could I do it? I asked myself these questions over and over, but nothing came to mind.

As I drifted off to sleep, all I could think about was money. I'd need money to start a business. If I could get some money, maybe I could buy an existing business.

The next day, I woke with a thrill of excitement. I hadn't been able to think of a single business idea yesterday when I was trying too hard, but today an idea appeared as if by magic. I'd do what I had done with Frank, but in a different field: I'd be a self-employed salesman for an established company. If I was a success, I'd save my money and start my own business.

Before I knew it, I was selling kitchens for a manufacturer that had a showroom. Having blagged my way in, I was offered a commission-only role.

The work was hard. I would have to travel for miles at my own expense, then design and sell a kitchen. If I didn't sell, I didn't earn. I had to close the sale on the day to be paid. Life wasn't what it used to be; gone was the luxury of an office round the corner. My car was now my office and I hated being on the road all the time. It was a horrible job, but if I sold, it paid well.

When I started earning again, there was one major change in me this time. Being so close to financial ruin had made me respect money. I no longer splashed the cash but saved every penny. I worked long hours, and in between jobs, I searched the internet for business opportunities. I was surviving, but not thriving;

I was tired and had put on weight. Living on the road meant junk food and Red Bull to keep me going. The gym membership expired and I didn't have the time to bother renewing it. How I longed for the days when I could relax in the sauna after a nice workout.

I wondered if Michelle was still going daily. She'd seemed focused and knew what she wanted. She was someone I wished I could talk to about how to make the switch from kitchen salesman to business owner. If I could be a little more like Michelle, then maybe I could figure out what to do.

Summary

The stock market crash of 2008 was a severe wake-up call for me and it seemed it couldn't have come at a worse time. But there is always a way through the hard times, and the mistakes we make and the knocks we suffer along the way leave us stronger. We just have to make sure we learn from them.

What did I learn from the lean times? Here's a recap:

- However much you're earning, it's never a good idea to splash the cash as if there is no tomorrow. There will be a tomorrow and you never know what it will bring. Savings that you can fall back on in times of trouble, or that you can invest in a career change, can be a blessing.

- No one is entitled to something for nothing. Instead of thinking in terms of what you should be earning, look at what you could earn.

- Whatever you think you can do, you can do, but be realistic. You may not play football in the Premier League, for example, but could you play for your local team?

- We are all what we think we are, so be mindful of your thoughts. If you think you are a failure, you will be. If you think you are a success, you will be. A good idea is to write down any negative thoughts you have, then change them to a more positive point of view. For example, replace 'I never have enough time' with 'I have so many opportunities, I need to decide what is best for me to move forward'.

- If you don't know what direction to take career-wise, list everything you're good at, and then everything you dislike doing. Then think about work that will incorporate as many items as possible on the first list while avoiding most of those on the second.

I had a job I hated and a dream for the future. Would my dream come true? Or were there a few hard knocks waiting for me before I'd get anywhere close?

Let's find out, shall we?

5

The Rise And Fall Of A Business Owner

The call came through at seven on Saturday morning, the start of a beautiful sunny day in 2010. It was the kitchen manufacturer, wanting to talk me into making a sale.

By this time, I was exhausted and couldn't take any more. I agreed to cover the appointment because it was too much effort to say no. The company had been let down and was reaching out to me for emergency cover.

The appointment was scheduled for 9am. Unfortunately, I fell back to sleep. I slept till early afternoon; the months of long days and travel had caught up with me. My unhealthy lifestyle had seen my fitness decline. But there was good news: I had savings for the first time in a long while and I'd secured a loan to fund the purchase of a small business. My search for a new career had come to an end.

My own business

I'd found a small company that offered care for elderly people in their own homes. Contracts were due for signing Monday morning, and I was excited and nervous in equal measures about starting my new venture. The company employed twelve people but was struggling and making a loss.

Homecare was an industry I knew nothing about. I had also never employed people before. While worried about leaving my comfort zone, I was confident I would be a good employer and turn the business around. I'd found an experienced manager to run the day-to-day operations and she would be starting on Tuesday, the day after I signed the contracts.

As my solicitor went through the main points of the contract, I pretended to listen while my mind wandered. Paperwork has always bored me; my attention has never been in the detail. All I needed were the basics. I remembered Ben, who would explain every last thing to his potential clients. How they must have suffered!

An hour or so later, I owned a business. I had a set of keys and would open up the next day. The excitement was immense. By now, I was full of energy and enthusiasm for my new business. I had so many hopes and dreams, it didn't matter to me that I had no idea how to run a homecare company. I knew why I wanted to do it and decided that was enough.

Why did I want to do it? I wanted to do something rewarding that would change other people's lives for the better. I could use my sales skills to win business and watch my care givers helping the elderly to have a better life. This was going to be amazing. And best of all, the industry I was entering would always be needed. Despite the economy being in a recession, there was an ageing population who would still pay for care when they needed it.

Also, I would finally be out of the rat race, just like Frank. My staff would work when I wasn't; I would earn money from their hard labour. It was exciting and I couldn't wait to get started.

My team

I met the team the next day. The previous owner had arranged for the field staff to visit the office to meet myself and Sally, my new office manager who was extremely experienced in care. I couldn't help but feel I had problems ahead. No one had anything nice to say about the company. The old owner had apparently run the business into the ground, and the staff felt mistreated, underpaid and unsupported.

At the end of the day, I was exhausted.

'All they did was moan,' I said to Sally as we locked up for the evening.

She looked right at me with a hint of anger in her eyes. 'Welcome to homecare,' she said sharply.

As the days and weeks passed, Sally did an amazing job with the staff. She knew everything that was going on and really seemed to care about the clients, laying down the law with any slackers on the payroll and telling them exactly what she expected. Unfortunately, she also laid down the law with me. Recognising that I was a weak leader, she had taken over. Conversely, a lot of work I would have expected her to do, she refused and handed over to me. She always seemed to be pushing for more money to buy something she claimed was essential or to cover an expense.

Why didn't I say anything? My lack of experience meant I didn't have the ability to manage the office, so I kept quiet. OK, I'll admit it: I was scared I'd upset her and lose her.

As the company started to do better, we picked up more work and got busier. This meant taking on more field staff and an office-based team member to organise the visits. Sally had said she couldn't cope with the logistics anymore and needed help, so I got her help. It was a shame, though, as we were just about making a profit, and now I'd have another salary to pay. As Olivia joined my team, I just hoped she would be good at her job.

Out of the frying pan...

I wasn't great with accounts; they confused me. In fact, I hated doing them. My accounting method was simple: money in the bank was good; no money in the bank meant panic. When I took Olivia on, I had no idea if the business could afford her or even really needed her. All I knew was that Sally had said she needed her, and what Sally wanted, she got.

As it happened, Olivia was good at her job. A plump lady with a cheery outlook on life, she liked to joke with me, often at her own expense.

'I'm only forty-five,' she'd say, 'but look at the lines on my face. This is what homecare does to you.'

Many a true word is spoken in jest. I had started to feel like the care industry was consuming me. As well as running the business and working every day, I had to make sure the on-call phone was covered so that staff and clients could phone at any time with an emergency that needed immediate attention. Of course, they needed to get through to a senior member of staff, and Sally point blank refused to have the phone. This meant I was manning it day and night, seven days a week. I could never switch off and was always busy.

What had happened to getting out of the rat race? Why couldn't I be like Frank? He was always so calm and happy, and I was working harder and harder. Business was growing, but the more it grew, the more out of control it became. More clients meant a busier on call and I was at breaking point. The dream of a nice income and freedom seemed miles away.

I was down and depressed. Life was hard and the enthusiasm I'd had for the business was leaving me. To make matters worse, problems had started at home. Debbie and I were always arguing, and I had taken to sleeping in the spare room. At first, I said this was so Debbie wouldn't be disturbed by the on-call phone ringing, but in reality, it was just convenient. My depression had an unfortunate side effect: I wasn't looking at Debbie in the way I used to, so she was feeling rejected. Add to that the fact I couldn't sleep for more than a few hours, which meant I was keeping her awake as well, and separate rooms seemed like the only answer.

Debbie had not changed over the years. She still worked part time and was an amazing mother, but she craved a normal life. A husband who worked nine to five Monday to Friday, a nice little house and a holiday with the kids every year was her dream, while I wanted a life of abundance and a big business that ran itself. Neither of us was getting what we wanted from the relationship, and more and more cracks appeared. People say that opposites attract, and for the majority of our relationship, it had worked well for us. However, they also say when money leaves the home, so does the love. It seemed there was neither love nor money in our home these days.

I started to feel alone. Debbie was a worrier; if she wasn't worrying about something, then she worried about not worrying. It was her nature, so I felt I couldn't talk to her. I loved her and didn't want to hurt her. But the worst thing I did was to bottle up all my problems and hide them from Debbie. The unhappier I became at work, the more I hid.

At work, Sally was pushing more and more on to me. All the staff, including me, were scared of her. Olivia seemed to be the only one I could trust. I often found myself taking refuge in her office and talking about different problems.

Despite my personal problems, my business was busy. We had a good reputation and the local authority had been giving us regular work, so I started to pay myself a modest salary. Financially, things were looking up.

Life, on the other hand, was chaotic and messy, and I was still hopeless with the accounts. The wages were always wrong, invoices were never paid on time, and when they were, the figure was lower than I'd expected. I had no idea how much money was owed and how well I was really doing. The business's bank account usually had money in it, so all was good in my mind.

Until it wasn't.

Into the fire

The council put all our invoices on hold, wanting to see time sheets for the whole month's visits before paying. Getting all this information was time consuming, but it had to be done. Without payment coming into the business, the staff's wages wouldn't be covered.

This was a disaster. What was I going to do? I was horrified as I hated letting people down. Care isn't a well-paid job and my carers worked hard. If I couldn't pay them, they would suffer. They would blame me; I would be hated. But the business would be £20,000 short if the council held payments. The stress was unbearable.

As I sat with Olivia, stressing over the unpaid invoices, I felt my chest tighten. I was in pain. Something was not right. I couldn't breathe and felt dizzy.

'You OK, Lee?' said Olivia. I shook my head. 'We need to get you to a hospital,' she went on, looking concerned as she jumped up and grabbed her car keys. 'You may be having a heart attack. Follow me.'

I don't remember getting to the hospital. I certainly don't remember how I ended up on the ward, strapped to a heart monitor. In the hospital reception area, I passed out. Apparently, Olivia caught me on the way down before I hit the floor.

As I came round, a pleasant young nurse was sitting in front of me.

'Don't panic, you are OK,' she said calmly. 'Everything is fine.'

'What happened?' I asked.

'You passed out and we put you in here.'

As I looked around, I wondered what had happened to me. Why was my life so bad? I work hard, so I should be a success. I should be like Frank. I didn't think I could take it anymore. Exhausted once again, I could only think negative and defeatist thoughts. The constant struggle of building a business and managing staff had become one giant mess. My life was in ruins. I was out of control and in debt. All I wanted was to shut the office door and never go back.

Debbie was looking after Annabelle when I got home. I looked at them both and wanted to cry. Working so hard to provide for them was tiring and I was failing. I never told Debbie of my suspected heart attack; she didn't even know I was in hospital that day. Just like everything else, I bottled it up, pretended everything was OK and tried to find a way to carry on.

Payday came and went. I made wages, but only just. Thankfully, the bank agreed an overdraft which took some of the immediate pressure off. At least if the council played games with the invoices again, I would have enough of a backup not to worry.

But the relief of the overdraft was short lived. The problem wasn't money. There was plenty of money, but it was badly managed, and it was sitting in other people's bank accounts. I wasn't getting paid on time because I had poor systems. My staff were taking advantage of me because I didn't manage them correctly. Everyone did what they thought they needed to do, not what they really needed to do because I had never taken the time to explain to anyone exactly what they should be doing.

Everything was left to chance. I was a person who dreamed big and had lots of ideas, but I didn't have the organisational skills to follow through and make them work. My staff had given up getting excited about my latest idea because they knew that I would forget about it and it would never come to fruition. I was spinning so many plates – the marketing plate, the accounts plate, the invoicing, staff issues, sales plate – and couldn't follow through on anything as I tried my best to control all areas of the business myself.

It wasn't the staff's fault when they sat back and let me run around like a headless chicken. It was mine, but I didn't know it yet. I still had the mentality I'd carried throughout my whole life: the harder you work, the more successful you will be. I had forgotten Frank's example, and the first lesson he'd taught me on asking for help. Instead, I took everything on myself, thinking no one would do a better job. I paid people to work but wouldn't let them. I wanted to control everything, and when things went wrong, I worked harder to sort the problem.

It seemed like I didn't fit in anywhere. I felt lost and lonely; life had become scary and depressing. I longed for my old life of selling mortgages and making lots of money. Things were relatively easy back then, even though I worked hard in the rat race. At least I had money. Nowadays, all I did was work hard to pay my staff, often going without myself when there was no money left at the end of the month. I was not enjoying life and had lost all the enthusiasm I'd once had for my business. I was at the end of my tether.

'What's the point of going on?' I asked myself.

Summary

This has been a rather sad chapter, but that was the way my life was heading in those days. The dream of running my own business had become a nightmare. Looking back, I can recognise all the things I was doing wrong, and I'm sure when you see the outcomes, you can too.

What would have been a better way of going about things? What would I have done differently? Here are a few hints:

- Have a really strong 'why' behind what you do. For me, it was providing a life of abundance for my family. It drove me to keep going, even when things got tough. Before I knew my why, I did things because I thought I had to, which led to boredom and depression.
  Knowing why you want to do something will help propel you to success.

- Sort problems out quickly and let people know where they stand. When everyone knows what is expected of them, the problems diminish. Never leave things and hope they will sort themselves out.

- If you feel uncomfortable doing something, ask yourself, 'Is the pain of doing it going to be worthwhile? Will it move me forward and be rewarding?' If the answer is yes, then go for it.

If not, ask someone else to do it. They will be rewarded for their work, and may actually be far better at the task than you are. Then you'll be free to do something that you will enjoy.

- Manage money well. If you don't enjoy accounts, get help. Don't leave things like I did, as this was the biggest contributing factor to my stress.

Asking for help when you need it is essential, just like Frank told me. Don't ever bottle your problems up. When I asked for help, people helped me and I thrived. Never be scared to ask for help, we all need it to be a success.

I had hit a low point in my life. Would there be a way out of it for me?

6
Work-life Imbalance

Everyone in my homecare business was excited to learn my wonderful news. I had spent weeks preparing a tender for local authority work and had been successful. This contract was huge: it meant we would be guaranteed homecare work if we performed well and would keep the company financially secure for years to come.

I'd entered an industry I knew nothing about and purchased a failing company. Within a year, I'd doubled turnover and was employing fifteen new members of staff. Having won this tender, I had the potential to put the company into the million-pound turnover range within just a few years.

On the outside, it looked like I was becoming the success I had always dreamed of being. Inside, I was dying a slow death. Every day, I had to force myself to go to work. I was exhausted, unhappy and confused, and worst of all, I had started to hate the very business I was relying on to deliver my dream.

The only positive was I could now pay myself a wage. Everything else seemed like a failure. The accounts were still a mess and I was spinning more plates than ever while allowing the staff to do whatever they wanted. Taking on more people just added to my problems. Most days, I felt like a therapist as they moaned about their lives while I tried to advise them on what to do to make things better.

The staff seemed to love coming into my office and talking to me. And to be fair, I enjoyed the escape from work as well, but the distraction led to more problems. I wasn't concentrating on the business and where it could be going. Every day, I was putting out fires, solving one problem only for another to pop up. Instead of going to Sally, the staff came to me. I was the least experienced person in the business, but I was always able to come up with a solution. It might not be the right solution, but I would never allow myself to admit that I simply didn't know.

Again, all this was my fault. I never implemented a system for solving problems, nor did I trust my employees to make decisions for themselves. It was no wonder I was exhausted.

Where is the fun?

My dream of a work-life balance tipped heavily in favour of life had vanished. My relationship with Debbie was in deep trouble. The easy life we'd once had was long gone, disappearing along with my dreams. I talked so much about other people's problems at work, by the time I got home, I was too mentally exhausted to pay any attention to my own.

It was a weird feeling. Physically, I was full of energy at the end of the day, but my mind was dead. I would go home and play with my daughter, trying to look as if I was paying attention, but the reality was I was thinking about work problems. The games were invariably cut short, either because of tiredness or due to the on-call phone ringing, forcing me to continue working. When Annabelle went to bed, I would watch TV as a way of dumbing my mind and escaping from reality.

Something had to give, and unfortunately it would be my relationship. The more I worked and the busier my company became, the more my mental health suffered. Debbie and I were still in separate bedrooms, both feeling very much alone. We had been together since we were young, and although we were experienced in the good times, we had no idea how to cope with the bad times. The relationship had been solid when there had been money, free time, holidays and romance. Now there was just stress, exhaustion and depression.

We both needed help but were too naïve to ask for it. I had lost friends, too, as I never had time for them anymore. They used to call to invite me out, but I always had to decline. It was no fun going out when the on-call phone was likely to ring at any moment, so it was easier not to go in the first place. In the end, my friends stopped calling. The fun I'd once had was lost. The only places I went were the office and home, and neither of those options was much fun these days.

Living life like this was taking its toll. I put on weight and looked older than I was. My hair started to thin due to the stress I was under, and wrinkles appeared on my face. Behind the smile I showed to the world was a man crumbling and scared. I was on the edge of despair and knew it.

Papering over the cracks

I still had the ability to think fast when I needed to and find temporary solutions to problems, but the problems were coming thick and fast. If only I had used my quick thinking for long-term planning.

Everything was short term with me because this was all I knew. Put out the fire, move to the next problem and repeat: I'd done this for so long, it had become a habit. I dragged myself through every day, slumping in my armchair in the evening. It had got so bad that I didn't even have the brainpower to watch TV. As Debbie fell asleep on the sofa every night, watching whatever she wanted, I would stare at the fish aimlessly swimming around in their tank.

Annabelle had bought me the fish tank for Christmas, and I loved it. The fish were beautiful and full of colour. As I watched, mesmerised, while they swam around and around, not getting anywhere, they reminded me of myself. I was doing the same, going around in circles and not getting anywhere. The fish's colourful scales matched my smile of false confidence; the tank was my large house. Just like the fish, I was living in a false environment: one I had created but had no control over.

The worst thing was that it had become normal, it had become my life. I no longer thought of Frank and his freedom; I had resigned myself to the life I had created. There was almost comfort in the chaos. I had money at the end of the month to pay the bills, and if the council paid my invoices, I would survive. I even took comfort in the realisation that I hated my business but looked like a success. Life was dull and boring, but I was too tired to do anything about it.

Maybe, I told myself, this is what business is really like.

As I scrolled through my social media feeds, though, I saw people talking about success and having a life of freedom and abundance. I wondered how they did it. Maybe they were lying. Maybe they were just luckier than me. I couldn't see any way out; I couldn't see how to make things better. I had no clarity over where I wanted my life and business to go. All I saw were problems.

Little did I know, my biggest problem so far was about to hit me.

Confrontation

I had been having problems with my arms for a while. It started with a tingling in my fingers; when I was driving, my hands would go numb and feel uncomfortable. When typing, I would experience the same tingling and would have to shake my hands to bring them back to life.

Over the next few months, things got worse. The numbness travelled through my arms, and I found it hard to lift them. Some evenings, I found it impossible to pick my daughter up. As usual, I put a brave face on and told no one, least of all Debbie, as I knew how sick with worry it would make her. Instead, I would come home, sit in my chair and stare at the fish, night after night, my arms tingling and aching at my sides. I couldn't be sick and take time off work; I had so much to do.

As I was thinking about the consequences of being off sick, Debbie walked into the room. She stood at the opposite end with her back pressed against the wall, staring at me with a look of dejection and sadness.

'You need to sort yourself out,' she said. 'You are going to make yourself ill.'

I felt a sense of rage well up within me as I heard these words. *I am ill*, I thought. *How can she not see it?*

'If you don't slow down, you will have a heart attack,' she added.

I have already been hospitalised with a suspected heart attack, I thought. Inside, I was raging, but I remained quiet.

'Say something,' she snapped.

'I *am* sick,' I blurted out. 'I can't move my arms; I can't get out of this chair. I need help, Debbie.'

I felt liberated at finally being honest with Debbie. I had pretended everything was OK for so long to protect her, never wanting to worry her in case it made her sick, so to get things out in the open was a relief.

The relief was short lived.

'What about me, Lee?' she fired back. 'You must sort your own problems, and then start paying me attention again. Where is the romance and the fun we once had?'

For the first time in our relationship, I lost my cool. An argument ensued and harsh words were said on both sides. Finally, Debbie left the room. As she left, I shouted after her that I would be leaving the family home and going to live somewhere else. If I had to sort out my problems on my own, I wanted to be alone. I thought leaving was the only logical solution. I needed space, and quickly. Debbie was right: I would have a heart attack if I carried on the way I was, and extra stress at home was not helping.

I tried to push myself up from the sofa, but my arms were not working. It was like I was paralysed and unable to control my body. I was angry with Debbie, unable to see that it was my fault she hadn't realised how much my health was suffering. She wasn't a mind reader, and I had been pretending everything was OK. It seemed I'd fooled everyone, even Debbie. All she had believed was that I had lost interest in her. My home life was on as much of a downward spiral as my work life. By not talking and being honest, by not asking for help, I'd created a huge mess.

Now, I believed my only way out was to leave Debbie and sort everything out myself. I would do what I had always done. I drifted off on the sofa, unable to move, and slept there all night.

By morning, thankfully, the rest had given life back to my arms and I could get up. I was out early that morning; I didn't want confrontation and took refuge at the office. The day was spent scrolling through Rightmove, searching for properties to rent. As I looked at the flats, I felt a sense of relief. If only I could change my circumstances, I might be able to change both Debbie's life and mine for the better. If I got out of the family home for a while, had some space to think, I could work everything out. Life would be good again.

Always one for making quick decisions, I fired off some enquiries about flats. 'Decide on it and see how it goes' had become my motto.

Lies, lies and more lies

As I shut down the PC, I heard my name mentioned in the main office. It was a man's voice and he sounded like someone of authority. Then Olivia came in and summoned me.

'There's someone here from Her Majesty's Revenue and Customs (HMRC) wanting to see you,' she said. My heart sank as I knew I was behind with the pay as you earn (PAYE) and national insurance contribution (NIC) payments. I hadn't expected it to be a problem, but a problem it was.

As I walked into the main office, the gentleman waiting for me announced for the whole office to hear that I hadn't kept up with contributions and owed £15,000 – and that it needed to be paid today.

Instantly, I felt my chest tighten and my arms go numb. I ushered him into my office for privacy and proceeded to tell him a sob story. Despite his loud voice and lack of tact, the HMRC inspector was actually quite pleasant. He listened to the story and seemed to sympathise.

As he sat with me and looked through the company bank statements, he agreed to take part payment now. After we'd devised a payment plan for the remainder, he left. As I walked through the main office, I could feel all eyes on me. The staff clearly sensed trouble.

Sally came into my office, fuming. 'Why was he here?' she said. 'What's going on? Are we in trouble, Lee?'

As ever, I hid the truth. 'Don't worry, Sally, everything is fine,' I lied. 'It was just a misunderstanding. I've been paying the money but used the wrong reference number. The inspector said he will sort it out.'

Sally wasn't convinced; the damage had been done. She left my office with a sceptical expression on her face and returned to her desk. Within weeks, she had left the company because, as she eloquently explained to the whole office, she didn't want to be on board a sinking ship.

As I sat in my chair with my head in my hands, I pondered on how my home life was in ruins and my staff didn't trust me. How had I got to the point where I was lying to everyone? I was spiralling out of control faster than ever.

The next day, I woke in my new flat with a sense of confusion. How had I ended up alone? What had my life become? As I walked into my new living area, I opened the curtains to look at a completely new view. I was used to looking out on to a large rear garden with beautiful trees and plants; now, I looked over a small balcony to the other flats in the block.

I felt a wave of emotion come over me as I sat on the armchair and looked down at the floor. For the first time in years, I cried. I sobbed and sobbed until I had no more tears left.

As it turned out, this burst of emotion was cathartic. This was the start of a new life. Getting my sadness out was what I needed. As I left for work, I didn't know how to make the changes I had to make; I just knew that I would.

Summary

Nothing in my life was how I had envisioned it would be. I'd thought business would be easy, people would work for me and I would get rich. I had dreamed of a lovely life with Debbie and Annabelle, but in truth, it was far from that. Working for my staff rather than the other way round, I couldn't give my family the life they deserved and felt like a failure.

By the time the tax man came knocking at the door, my relationship was in tatters and my health was hanging by a thread. The finances were a mess, the office was a mess. In my muddled mind, the only way out was to move into a flat on my own, get some rest and work out a plan.

But the hard times are essential in our lives, as without them we can't learn and grow. If times are hard for you at the moment, don't despair. Things will get better, as long as you learn from your mistakes, identify and make the changes you need to make and, of course, ask for help when you need it.

Here's a summary of the learnings I took from this terrible time:

- Take control of situations before they take control of you. When you deal with problems properly and the people around you know what to expect and do, life will become easier and less stressful. And if you don't know the answer to a problem, ask for help. Even simply talking it over can clear your mind, which can only be a good thing as you work towards a solution.

- Long-term planning always trumps short-term solutions. A quick fix can work wonders, but when life is full of quick fixes, it becomes tiring and stressful. Plan for the long term, and then break your plans down into small chunks to make them easier to manage. Set daily tasks to make sure you keep on track and complete all your plans.

- People can't read your mind, so don't expect them to. Don't pretend to have everything under control if it's not; be open and honest with people, and they will usually want to help. Life is easier when you have lots of help.

I'd got to the point where I'd recognised the need for change, but would I be able to identify the key changes I had to make? And would I actually make them?

7
Gaining Clarity

Before entering the office, I took a deep breath and composed myself. *No one can know what is going on at home*, I told myself as I walked through the main door.

I'd become a master of keeping my problems to myself. Telling others what I was going through was something I considered a weakness. If I was seen as vulnerable, people would take advantage. Business is tough and only the strong survive.

I was surviving, but just, making enough money to look after Debbie and Annabelle and pay for my flat, and nothing more. I was living on a tightrope, hoping the business invoices would be paid and there would be enough money to pay the bills. In a way, Sally leaving was a good thing. I had basically been doing her job anyway, so not having her salary helped financially, but I needed a manager. It is a legal requirement to have a registered care manager within a homecare company and I wasn't qualified. I would be OK to run things for a short while, but I had to find someone soon.

One member of staff, Kate, had been with me for a short while. Young and pretty with long straight hair and a smiley face, Kate was smart not just in appearance, but mentally. She cared about the clients, which was important, but she also seemed to care about the staff.

Since Sally had left, Kate had stepped up naturally and taken on some responsibility. Could I ask her for help while I was looking for a new manager? Would she be prepared to share the burden?

A face from the past

Procrastination had become my middle name. Instead of exploring this possibility, I fired up my PC. While flipping through a digital edition of the local newspaper, I saw a face I recognised: Michelle, the woman I had met in the gym. Looking elegant and happy, she was sitting in a big chair like Frank's, a sparkling smile across her face. The headline above the picture said,

'Local Retiree Now One of the UK's Most Successful Business Coaches'.

I felt a surge of excitement as I knew this lovely woman, who had been such a help to me in the past. I read the article, which went on to explain that Michelle had run a successful recruitment agency for many years before selling it five years ago. Bored and lonely after losing her husband, she started to coach small business owners as a hobby. The story said that she'd enjoyed it so much, she decided to open a coaching business.

At the end of the article, the reporter had posed a question to Michelle: 'What would you say is the biggest challenge most business owners have?'

'Lack of clarity,' Michelle had responded. 'Most business owners I coach have very little idea where they are taking the business or what they want to achieve. They spend so much time working out *how* to do things; they don't focus on *what* needs doing or *why* they want to do it.' Michelle went on to explain that she could help people get clarity on where their businesses were going to take away the confusion and stress.

Michelle looked so happy and free, just like Frank. That made me think about him and my dream to emulate him. *Maybe clarity is their secret,* I thought. *Maybe it's clarity that sets them free.*

I took a minute to think about what I wanted, gazing at my PC, my mind in dreamland. After a while, I gave up; my thoughts kept wandering to my daughter, Annabelle. All I really wanted was to see her. I missed her very much and would have given everything up to have my little girl living with me. The business seemed insignificant, and I had no idea what to do with it. I was no nearer to gaining the clarity that Michelle had said was all important.

Maybe I should just sell up and do something else. The company was a mess, I was a mess, so maybe it was time to let someone take over. But as I thought of selling, I reminded myself that not only did I pay for the house Debbie and Annabelle lived in, I had to pay my rent. How would I afford all this if I sold? What would I do for work? What would happen?

I had no idea. I had absolutely no clarity whatsoever. Maybe I should call Michelle for help. But that was a massive step. Despite Frank's advice, I wasn't used to asking for help and still saw it as a weakness. I was the boss and should make the decisions, not some coach who knew nothing about me.

I'll just speak with Michelle, I reassured myself. *She can tell me what I need to do, then I can leave and do it.* That was my thinking. I knew nothing about coaching; as far as I was concerned, only sports stars had coaches, and as I'm sure you've guessed by now, my childhood dream of being a professional footballer for Arsenal was long behind me, so why would I need a coach? I fired off an email and reminded Michelle of the time we had met at the gym, telling her I wanted her to show me how to get clarity and asking when she was free.

The brutal truth

After sending the email, I entered the main office. To my satisfaction, it was buzzing with efficiency, so I decided to treat myself to a day off. Walking to the exit, I bumped into Kate.

'Where are you off to?' she asked.

'Erm, I'm going home,' I said, feeling slightly embarrassed. I needn't have worried.

'OK, great, have a lovely time,' Kate said, looking happy and relaxed as she returned to the main office. And that's when I came to one of my quick decisions. I would ask for her opinion.

'Kate, before I go, can we have a quick word in private?'

'Whassup?' Kate asked chirpily as we entered my office and closed the door behind us.

'The staff seem different today,' I replied. 'People seem happy and they are all working. No one has moaned to me or demanded anything.'

'Yes,' said Kate, 'it's been like that since Sally left. You paid her to manage, but you did everything. We all hated seeing you like that. It wasn't fair, so make sure whoever you bring in to manage the office in her place does their job. The staff will turn again if the same thing happens, and you will lose all their respect.'

'Thank you for the honesty, Kate. I appreciate it and I'll see you tomorrow. I think things are changing for us and will be getting a lot better.'

'I hope so,' Kate replied. 'Some of the staff have mentioned leaving. I hope they don't, but you never know.'

Kate turned and walked into the main office as I froze with fear. *What if my staff leave? What will I do? I can't manage this on my own, I'll lose everything.* I had just lost Sally, Debbie and Annabelle, and now the remainder of my staff might leave too. The little glimpse I'd had of an office working efficiently and happily was crushed by an image that entered my head of everyone leaving me. The thought saddened me. I instantly felt depressed, missing Annabelle more than ever.

My coaching begins

On Saturday morning a week or so after my chat with Kate, I was sitting at my desk, watching email notifications pop up. I hadn't checked my emails for some time, so there were many to go through. Then I noticed a reply from Michelle. I couldn't resist looking at that one before any of the others.

'I remember you well, Lee,' it said. 'You had just lost your mortgage business, if I remember correctly? I would definitely be able to help you, so I suggest we start with a forty-five-minute discovery session to see if we can work together. I won't charge for this, and afterwards you can decide in your own time whether to use my services.

'I have Tuesday 3 June at 3pm free, so let me know if that suits you,

'Michelle.'

That's this Tuesday, I thought. Before I could chicken out, I fired off a reply to say I would be happy to take that appointment. Then I waited. It was Monday morning before Michelle replied, confirming the appointment, giving me her address and asking me to let her know if I couldn't make it.

I was excited to be meeting Michelle again. If my staff were going to leave me, I needed her to tell me what to do. I didn't want to lose the business, but at this stage I didn't have a clue whether to sell it or grow it. Michelle would make everything right.

I went to bed the night before my meeting a happy man, sure Michelle would have the answers. For the first time in a long while, I had a good night's sleep.

At the time of the meeting, I arrived at Michelle's home. She had a lovely house on a sought-after street not far from where I had lived with Debbie. Michelle took me to a spare room which was now her office and offered me a cup of coffee. Then we were ready to begin.

'Tell me, Lee, what do you know about coaching?' she asked.

'Well, you tell me what to do and I go away and do it,' I replied. 'If I do it well, I sort myself out, and if not, you tell me what I did wrong so I can get it right.'

'Well, it's not exactly like that. What do you think is wrong in your business?'

'How long have we got?' I joked. 'There's so much wrong, you will have a tough job fixing me.'

'What if I showed you that you are not broken and not in need of fixing? What if I showed you that you have all the answers within you, and it will be you who shows you what you need to do? How could that benefit you, Lee?'

I told her how great that sounded, how I would love to have the answers. I had hoped Michelle would tell me what to do but recognised that if I came up with the answers myself, it would be even better. I didn't like being told what to do anyway, so this coaching thing sounded OK.

'What does your perfect life look like to you?' Michelle asked. 'Both personally and in business?'

I looked up at the ceiling as if inspiration would be there. It wasn't something I'd ever thought about.

'I want my business to do well and make more money. I want to be happy and not work so hard. I want to spend more time with my daughter and have fun. I want to be free.'

'Tell me more about being free,' Michelle said.

'I feel like I am tied to my work. I cannot breathe or escape it. I'm scared something will go wrong and my staff will leave. I want to take on more work, but the more I take on, the more hassle I have. Life is a mess. I'm so unhappy that I can't see my daughter as much as I used to. It gets me down and I can't snap out of it.' I could have said so much more but was conscious I'd let my guard down. I'd opened up and wasn't sure if it was the right thing to do, so I sat quietly until Michelle spoke.

'Do you see what you just did, Lee? I asked you to tell me more about being free and you told me about all the problems you have, what you can't do, the hassle you have, how you miss your daughter. Not once did you mention anything about being free.'

I thought for a while. 'You are right,' I said. 'I am focusing on the negatives.'

In that moment, I had the realisation that most of my thoughts these days were negative. I was sad about not seeing Annabelle and tired from constantly working. Gone were the times when I wanted what Frank had; I couldn't even remember those days anymore. I'd given up; I was living, but just. There was no positivity or excitement left. I seemed to have no purpose in life.

'What can I do to change?' I asked Michelle.

'What do you want to change, Lee?'

'I want to be positive; I want energy and enthusiasm for life. I want my business to be better and my life to be better. That's what I want.'

'On a scale of one to ten, how committed are you to changing?'

'Ten. I want to do it, I need to do it,' I almost shouted with excitement.

Michelle went on to tell me her charges and we agreed to see each other every week for a total of five sessions. I left Michelle's home with a spring in my step having just taken a massive leap forward. I'd finally asked for help – and it felt good. For the first time in a long while, I was happy with myself. Michelle was going to coach me to change my life and business for the better.

The sessions with Michelle would become the highlight of my week. I didn't know it at this stage, but what I would discover would be life changing.

Summary

Michelle knew I wasn't broken. She knew that I had everything I needed inside me to gain clarity and make key changes. All she would do was draw my power out so I could use it to change anything I wanted in life. And best of all, Michelle knew exactly how she was going to do this.

I was sure I was going to become a new man, full of energy and confidence. Michelle cared passionately about her clients and guiding them to make the changes they wanted. I was Michelle's latest client and there was no way she would let me down.

Quite simply, gaining clarity on what you want in life and business is the best thing you can ever do. When you have clarity, you know exactly what you want and can plan to get it.

Here is a great piece of advice around clarity:

• List everything you want to achieve in life – be precise and descriptive. The more detail you write, the better. Take time to think and feel what you desire coming true. Write it as if you have already achieved it, for example, 'The date is (sometime in the future). I have a big white house which is double fronted and approached via a long driveway'.

• When you can really visualise what you want, you start to gain clarity on it. Then the ideas will come on what you need to do to achieve it.

Life was finally looking up for me. Frank had been right all along: all I had to do was ask for help, and help would be forthcoming. And asking Michelle for help was going to be the best decision I had ever made, in both life and business.

8
Being Coached

Michelle and I met on a Friday morning after her gym workout. I wanted an earlier appointment, but she flatly refused.

'Nothing gets in the way of what I want to achieve, Lee,' she explained. 'I have a clear vision for my life and a plan to make everything happen. These days, staying fit and healthy is a priority of mine, so exercise is especially important. I can see you just after, but certainly not before my morning workout.'

I admired her honesty and dedication. It wasn't by luck that she looked so good for her age. I, on the other hand, looked much older than I was. The last few years had been tough; I no longer went to the gym and had put on weight. The clothes I once took so much pride in wearing didn't fit anymore. I hadn't noticed the weight creeping up silently and sneakily like a ninja, until boom! It was all over me, and I had no idea how it had got there.

Of course, I knew in my heart I had let myself go. Fitness was no longer important to me; I wore baggier clothes to hide my expanding tummy and told myself I still looked good. Every now and then, I would catch a glimpse in a car or shop window as I walked past and feel ashamed. I told myself I would get back to the gym, but there was never time or I was too tired to train. The little energy I had was used at work. The remainder of the day, I spent watching TV on my own. The only excitement in my life was when my daughter Annabelle visited and stayed for the weekend.

I have to change, I thought while sitting in the small but comfortable armchair at Michelle's house. Our first official coaching session was about to start, and I was nervous.

My first session

'OK, Lee,' Michelle broke the silence, 'what do you want to work on today?'

'I read your article on clarity,' I replied. 'I want what you have: I want to be focused and know where I am going. I want to be happy and have more free time. I want to be a better dad and enjoy my life. If you can help me with all of that, I'll be very grateful.'

'All of that is good, Lee. Tell me what your life is like right now.'

I took a deep breath and wondered how much I should tell Michelle. Then I foolishly decided to embellish the truth slightly, just give her the parts I thought I needed help with. Michelle looked strong and in control, so I didn't want to look weak in front of her.

'Life is good,' I said. 'I have a great care business with lots of motivated staff, I have a lovely daughter from a previous relationship, and I now live alone. I miss my daughter, which makes me sad, but generally I am happy. But I would like to be happier, and I would like to grow my business as well.'

Michelle thought for a while, then she told me she sensed I was holding back. She remembered the discovery session where I had told her many of the things that were wrong in my life and had stated she would have a tough job fixing me. From that meeting, she said, she had gathered my business was in trouble or something wasn't quite right. We needed to explore this further.

'What's the current situation with your business and staff?' she asked.

It was my turn to think for a while, my mind wandering back to the discovery session. What had I told her? I couldn't remember; I was so busy these days, I tended to forget many things.

'It's a homecare business,' I replied eventually. 'I have grown the business and taken on more staff. It pays the bills, but it's a hard company to run. I do OK, but that's about it.'

'OK,' said Michelle, 'sounds good. Tell me more about what the business looks like now.'

'It's hectic,' I said. 'I employ a lot of people, which is a challenge. Managing a lot of staff causes problems as everyone wants different things, so I have to work long hours. There is plenty of work and I have no problem growing the business; the only thing that holds me back is getting enough staff.'

'What was the business like before?'

'It was pretty much the same, just smaller. I had fewer people to deal with. Staffing was still a problem, but it always seems to be a problem. I'm not sure much can be done; it's just the way it is.'

As my words drifted into silence, I felt my energy and demeanour change. Michelle must have noticed as she decided to push for more information.

'Tell me about the situation with your staff, Lee.'

I sat up straight, put on a brave face and spoke of how great the staff were and how hard they worked. I told Michelle of the stressful job they had and all the things they had to do to keep the company going. I talked about Sally leaving and how I'd found her impossible to manage.

Michelle thought briefly, then replied, 'What I'm hearing, Lee, is that you have a great business that pays the bills. You employ a lot of staff, but some of them can be challenging. Have I understood correctly?'

'Yes, that's right. If it wasn't for the staff, the business would be great,' I joked.

I talked for what seemed like hours about my staff and the problems I had. My guard had dropped a little and I felt safe in taking Michelle into my confidence. There was something about her I trusted, and it felt good to get things out in the open.

'When Sally left, how did you feel?' asked Michelle.

I was on a roll and told her how hurt I had been. 'I had a problem paying the PAYE and NIC, then an inspector from HMRC came and demanded money. Sally knew I was in trouble and jumped ship, telling the whole office why she was leaving. I was embarrassed and really upset.'

'What happened next, Lee?'

'I've stepped in as office manager until I can get some-one else. It's OK, but it's not what I want to do.'

'How has the business changed since you took over?'

'Like I said, it's OK. I get things done. The staff do what I need them to do and we tick over. In some ways, it seems better. I even took a day off recently, which was nice.'

'Tell me more about that,' Michelle said excitedly.

My energy picked up as I told her about my chat with Kate before I left the office that day. 'She seemed happy for me to take some time off,' I said. 'She seems different, and she's taken on more responsibility with-out even being asked to. When I took the rest of that day off, it felt good. Nothing bad happened at work. It was a nice day, to be honest.'

As I spoke, I felt a wave of sadness come over me. Days off and the office running well without me were what I wanted more of, but I wasn't confident enough to tell Michelle this just yet. For me to admit things were out of control would be a sign of weakness. I felt trapped. Deep down, I knew Kate was perfectly capable of giving me the help I needed, but I couldn't let go. I was doing as I'd always done and bottling everything up.

Getting to the truth

The coaching session carried on and Michelle asked a host of open questions for me to ponder over and answer. I sensed she knew what was wrong and pushed back, pretending everything was OK and skirting around the truth. It felt good to be talking to someone in confidence, but no way was I going to look weak in front of Michelle.

Then Michelle asked a simple question that caught me off guard. 'If you had a magic wand and could change anything in your business, what would it be?'

Before I could stop myself, I had blurted out, 'The business would run well without me every day.'

'Interesting,' said Michelle. 'Tell me more.'

Damn, why did I say that? I thought. My reaction was to backtrack. If I was honest with Michelle, she would find out that my staff did what they wanted, when they wanted, while I ran around all day putting out fires. I didn't want her to know that, so changed the subject, telling Michelle how great the business was and my plans for the future.

Undeterred, Michelle ignored my spiel and asked me what a business that ran itself looked like to me. I realised I was going to have to give her more.

'I used to work with a guy called Frank, who had a business that ran itself,' I said. 'He hired freelance mortgage brokers who did all of the work. Frank would take a cut of their commission and do a little business himself on the side. He didn't spend much time at the office, we hardly ever saw him, but he had a great life and always seemed happy.'

'That's interesting. Tell me, Lee, for you to achieve what Frank had, what actions would you need to take?'

'I don't know. I don't think it's possible in my business; in a care company, we have to work all the time. It's expected of us. I can't see me ever being able to step away from the business and be like Frank. It's not possible.'

'How many people are like Frank, do you think?' Michelle asked. 'How many have a business that runs without them?'

She wasn't going to catch me out that easily. 'I see what you are doing, but you don't understand care. This business is different. We are dealing with people's lives and we have to be on call all the time. As individuals, we don't get many days off and we are always on the go. It would be impossible to run the business and not be there. The staff wouldn't know what to do and I wouldn't be able to help them when things go wrong.'

Michelle sat in silence as I finished speaking and I wondered if I had said the right thing. Could I actually have what Frank had? It was my dream to be free and have a successful business that ran without me, so what was holding me back? Why was I failing and so unhappy with my life?

Making progress

'What are you thinking, Lee?' Michelle's gentle voice broke into my thoughts.

'Erm, just that it would be nice to have some free time. We are busy and the company is doing well, but I'd like more time with my daughter and to be able to enjoy life more.'

'What can you do to give yourself free time?'

'I really don't know,' I replied. 'I need a new manager. I have to have someone Care Quality Commission registered as a legal requirement. Maybe when I find that person, I can take a day off here and there.'

'How would having a new manager help you take some time off?'

'They could take on some of my work, and when I have less to do, I could use the time that frees up for leisure.'

'How does it feel, the idea of having someone to ease your workload and free you up for leisure time?'

'Feels good,' I said with a smile on my face. 'I like the sound of that.'

'So, what actions do you need to take to employ someone and give them some of your work?'

I let myself dream for a while about a new manager taking work from me. I thought about how great it would be and the positive impact it would have on my life.

'I could advertise for someone, making sure I specify what I want them to do,' I replied after a while. 'I can include some of my work in their job description and show them how to do it when they start.'

'What do you feel when you think of having a manager who takes work away from you?' she asked.

'I feel good,' I replied. 'It could work. I deserve some time off, and if I can get the right person to help me, that would be great.'

'That would be great,' Michelle repeated with a huge smile on her face. 'What would be especially great about it?'

'I could spend time with Annabelle; I could have fun; I could do things I want to do instead of working all the time.'

'Lee, tell me something. Let's say you employ a new manager and they remove some of the workload from you. What does your company look like then?'

I thought for a while and pushed back. 'Not that different. I'll have a day off here and there, which will be nice, but the company won't change. We will still be doing the same stuff.' I had so much sadness and disappointment within me, I was frightened to let go. If I did, I might get emotional and break down. I was used to bottling everything up; I knew no other way.

If I broke down and cried, would Michelle think I was weak? Would she judge me and look on me as not being a real man? There was something different about her. She didn't appear to be judgemental at all; she never gave an opinion or said my replies were wrong; she just asked questions. The questions were sometimes uncomfortable to answer, but I felt safe in Michelle's office in her home.

'I think getting someone in is a good idea,' I said.

'Tell me, Lee, what would the situation be if this person came in and made a massive difference to your business, giving you the freedom you want?'

'That would be amazing! I would be able to do so much more: spend quality time with Annabelle and friends; go on holiday; lie in bed all day if I wanted. Life would be great.' I lifted my head to the ceiling as if to pray for all this to happen, then let out a sigh of relief as I imagined how my life and business could be.

'Lee, our session is ending soon. What do you think you will do when you leave here?'

For the first time that morning, I felt decisive. 'I am going to get someone to manage the office for me,' I replied. 'I will give them some of my work to free my time up a bit. Then I will do less work myself and get my manager to do it instead.'

'How does that feel?'

'It feels good. I know I can afford someone; I just need to find the right person.'

I left the session feeling optimistic. It hadn't been what I'd expected, but I was happy to have been able to talk to someone. I had made a little progress and, more importantly to me at the time, I hadn't looked weak in front of Michelle.

It had been a good day and I had an idea of what to do to make things better.

Summary

I went into my first coaching session with Michelle willing to open up, but only so much. The most important thing for me at the time was to make sure I didn't look weak in front of this strong woman. But despite the defences I had put up, her skill ensured that we did make progress.

What did I learn during our conversation? Here's a quick recap:

- There are always options. It took coaching to open my eyes to this, but the fact was I didn't need to take all the workload of running my business on my own shoulders. All I had to do was find the right person to manage my business, and make sure I was clear on what I expected them to do. Yet again, Frank's advice had been proved right.

- Never let misconceptions about image stop you from seeking help where you need it. If someone is going to view you as weak for asking for help, the likelihood is they're a toxic influence in your life anyway. Both good and bad people will come and go throughout life. Don't waste time with people who are no good for you or your goals. Replace them with people who will help you. Surround yourself with supportive people and your life can only improve.

- Be clear on what you want. You'll know deep down what it is, and you may even know how to achieve it. If you don't, that support network will prove its worth yet again.

- Your health is important. I let myself go and put on weight, which did me no good either mentally or physically. Make time to look after yourself. Schedule it in your diary. It's that crucial. A healthy business owner is an efficient business owner, and efficiency will free up even more time.

I left my first coaching session with Michelle feeling a renewed sense of confidence. I had a plan to make my life better, but would I put that plan into action?

9
Facing Up To The Truth

Driving back to my office, I thought of my session with Michelle. It hadn't been what I was expecting, but I'd enjoyed it. The nearer I got to the office, though, the worse I felt. A sick feeling rose within me as I wondered what problems would be waiting.

When I walked into the office, my fears were realised. It was hectic and there was an atmosphere of stress hanging in the air. Some staff were panicking, others were proclaiming loudly how much they hated working for the company. Even Kate seemed on edge.

'What's wrong?' I asked, the sick feeling in my stomach getting worse as I anticipated the answer.

'Visits to cover and not enough staff,' Kate replied, and all around her I saw heads nodding in agreement. The looks of despair on everyone's faces affected me negatively. I hated seeing my staff stressed. All I wanted was for them to be able to do their jobs and be happy.

I sat in my chair, fired up the PC and started to work on the latest problem. The hint of optimism I had felt after the meeting with Michelle was replaced with the sick worried feeling I had become accustomed to.

A vision of happiness

As the day passed and the stress in the office subsided, I logged on to a recruitment site to place an advert for more care staff. I typed what I was looking for, added the job description and posted the advert. Hopefully, I would find some good workers and the staff would appreciate my efforts to help.

As I was about to close the browser, my eye was drawn to a section entitled 'CV search'. In no time, I found myself searching through care manager CVs, reading with interest the bios and work histories.

I wonder, I thought. *Should I interview some of these people to see what is out there?*

Making decisions has never been my weak point. Before I knew it, I'd fired off multiple emails, asking for more information. Then I shut down my PC and left to go home.

That night, as I sat alone in my new flat, I let my mind drift to imagine life with a business that gave me no problems. I envisioned a company that was a happy place to work. The staff would be pleased to be there every day and we'd all love the office vibe. The new manager running the show would be excellent, taking the stress away while helping me grow the business.

I hadn't dreamed for a long time; I was always too caught up in problems. As I lay on my sofa and immersed myself in the dream, I felt good. I loved watching my staff working happily and becoming successful. I was calm; I was finally succeeding.

As I came back to reality, I wondered if life could really be like that. My initial response was that it couldn't. It was just a dream, but an intriguing one. Then something inside disagreed with my pessimism. I had a tiny glimmer of hope that maybe it could. The optimism was faint, but definitely there.

Maybe there is something in this coaching business after all, I thought while drifting off to sleep.

Assessing my life

The next day was no different from any other. I awoke feeling sick with worry, showered, rushed my breakfast, dressed and left for work, wondering why the hell I bothered.

I was first in and took time to appreciate the calm before the storm. As I made coffee, my mind started to drift again. I wondered what the day would bring and hoped for a good one. As the staff turned up one by one, things were looking hopeful. People were bustling around and chatting, making drinks and discussing their evenings.

Then the PCs were switched on and the atmosphere changed as if by magic. From buzzing and happy, everyone became stressed and out of control. The phones were ringing constantly, and the staff struggled to cope with the volume of calls. Everyone was on the go and would be all day, never having a moment to stop and breathe.

As I observed this change in atmosphere, I wanted to pull the electricity plug to give everyone a break. *What would happen if I did?* I thought. Life would go on; the world wouldn't stop turning. I felt a surge of excitement coming over me. I so badly wanted to cut the power and see what would come next, but was scared I would never be able to turn it back on again.

Later that day, I pulled up on the big driveway of the house I'd shared with Debbie and Annabelle and sat for a moment to look at what I once had. The size of the house dwarfed the little flat I was living in.

Debbie greeted me with a smile, led me to the kitchen and disappeared to get Annabelle, but she didn't attempt to make conversation. As I sat alone, waiting, I realised it was unlikely I would ever move back in with Debbie. It seemed an age since I had been living there. The happy memories had faded and been replaced with sadness and despair.

My thoughts were interrupted by an excited voice echoing down the stairs.

'Daddy!' Annabelle shouted as she ran into the room and greeted me. 'I've missed you so much.'

I felt a wave of emotion come over me; I had missed her too and was excited to see her. Annabelle and I seemed to be the biggest losers within the whole mess of separation. I worried how she would cope and what the effects would be on her long term. The sadness I held within wasn't helping me personally or at work. More and more, I was focusing on the negatives.

I gave Annabelle a huge hug. As we embraced, I told her of the lovely plans I had for our time together. She would be sleeping over tonight and we'd have a whole day together tomorrow.

'Can't wait,' she replied as we left the house for our adventure. But there was something I needed to do first.

'I've got to pop into the office,' I explained. 'Daddy just needs to check something, and then we can go to the cinema.'

'OK, Daddy,' Annabelle replied cheerfully. She liked being at the office, telling me it made her feel close to me.

As we drove, Annabelle informed me about all the fun things she had done at school and with Debbie since she had last seen me. I nodded and agreed when I thought it was necessary, but I wasn't really listening. My mind was full of problems and the awkward conversations I needed to have with members of staff. Over and over, I tried to anticipate what they would say so I could perfect my answer. It was exhausting, but it was a habit I couldn't stop. When people did talk to me, I never really listened. My attention was always elsewhere or buried in my mobile phone.

Today was no different. Even though I was supposed to be enjoying time with Annabelle, my mind was at work in one form or another. Never switching off or appreciating what I had, I was missing out on so much, and I knew it – but could I stop it?

Now was as good a time as any to try.

'You know what, Annabelle, let's skip the office and go and have some fun,' I said, more to make up for not listening than anything else.

'YES!' she screamed.

As I turned the car and drove away from the office, I couldn't help feeling fearful. What if something urgent needed doing? What if some care staff hadn't shown up for their jobs? Who would sort it out? Once again, I was disappearing into my own little world where problems presented themselves and I worked on sorting them out one by one. Only when I was satisfied I had the answers to deal with each problem quickly if it arose did I allow myself to focus on Annabelle again.

The day actually ended up being a good one. For the majority of the time, I managed to block out my problems and worries about work.

I wish I could be a kid again and start all over, I thought as I watched Annabelle playing. *If only I knew back then what I know now, things would be so much better.* I would have a great relationship with Debbie, I wouldn't be a part-time dad and I would have an awesome business that ran itself without me. Life would be good and I'd be so happy.

The fear of change

As Annabelle continued playing, I envisioned life being different and drifted into my own little world again. It was a world where I could sort problems by rehearsing speeches, a world where I was happy. I longed for it to be my reality.

Then I started to feel angry about life and all the bad things that were happening to me. Instead of getting better since the first session with Michelle, my life seemed to have got worse. I had allowed myself to dream a little since that session. The dreams were positive and nice while they lasted, but reality was different. When I focused on problems, I knew what to expect and how to deal with them. When I dreamed nice things, I was only setting myself up for disappointment when these things failed to happen.

Maybe this coaching thing isn't for me after all, I thought. *All this woo-woo talk and imagining a better life, but nothing has changed. I see Annabelle, have a lovely time, then get depressed when I have to say goodbye. Life is awful; no one's happy. It's the same everywhere. It's just the lucky few who make it and I'm not one of them.*

I had decided to cancel my session with Michelle by the time I dropped Annabelle back to Debbie's at the end of our weekend together. Then I remembered I had already paid for the five sessions. I might have been sad and depressed, but I wasn't about to throw good money away.

I'll give it one more go, and then quit if things don't improve, I decided. But as I sat in Michelle's chair at our next session, I felt angry and frustrated.

'This isn't working,' I said abruptly, going on to tell her how nothing had changed at work, I was still depressed and lonely. I'd hoped she would fix me, but she hadn't. In fact, she'd made things worse.

As I got everything off my chest, I felt better. I had given it to Michelle straight and told her how it was.

'I'd like a refund,' I said.

'I can arrange that,' Michelle replied, 'but first, can I ask how long you have had these problems?'

'Years,' I said. 'Ever since I bought that bloody company. I hate it! I hate being there and what it does to me. It's horrible and I want to get rid of it.'

Michelle thought for a while, and then replied, 'I sense a lot of anger within you, which has built up over the years, not just since you bought the company. You've paid for five sessions with me, Lee. Did you really expect to find the answers to years' worth of problems in one session?'

I didn't want to answer. I knew I was a long way off working out what I needed to do, but I was scared to make changes. After sending emails to prospective managers, as usual, I hadn't followed through. I knew some candidates had replied, but I hadn't read their messages. I wanted to let go, but at the same time, I craved the familiarity of not letting go. I was so confused, the clarity I was seeking seemed further away than ever.

Instead, I dodged the question and told Michelle a long story about emailing new managers but having been too busy to respond to their replies yet. I went on to say I felt sick every day and all I could think about was selling the business.

'What would life be like if you sold the business today?' Michelle asked.

I told Michelle I didn't really want to sell. The business was a mess and no one would buy it anyway, or if they did, they would pay next to nothing for it. Confusion took me over. I wanted to sell, and then I didn't. One minute I wanted to fix it, the next I couldn't be bothered.

'I'm just really fed up,' I said. 'I don't know what to do.' I then described what my ideal business would look like. I told Michelle once again about how happy everyone would be and what a lovely company it would be to work for. I would have as much time off as I wanted, knowing I had a great manager in place to run things. As I spoke the words, I felt happier and more at ease. The anger left my body and I relaxed.

'What do I do?' I asked Michelle.

'That's a good question. What do you think you should do?' she replied. With that, my anger returned. I ranted at Michelle that I was paying her to tell me what to do and if I knew all the answers, I wouldn't need her. I told her in no uncertain terms that I was disappointed. She had not helped at all.

The truth is out

Inside, I knew I was blaming her out of desperation. It was down to me to change, but I didn't yet believe I could. I hadn't acted on the emails from potential new managers, and I was letting my staff walk all over me. All of this made me feel less of a man.

And to make matters worse, I thought angrily, wanting to deflect the blame away from myself, *there's this woman sitting in front of me, taking my money and telling me to sort my own mess out. Unbelievable.*

'You've told me how great life could be, Lee,' said Michelle calmly. 'Tell me what your life is like now.'

'Bloody horrible,' I replied, not holding back. If she wanted to know, I would let her know. All the anger, frustration and sadness poured out of me as I told her of my situation. I spoke and spoke, almost without breathing, and Michelle listened to every word.

When I'd finished, we both sat in silence. I reflected on what I'd said and found to my surprise I felt calmer. The anger was out and I was relieved. For the first time in a long while, I had been honest with someone, and it felt good.

After what seemed an age, Michelle broke the silence. 'Tell me, Lee, what will your life be like if you don't commit to making changes?'

I felt exposed by Michelle's words. I had battled to keep things from her and embellish the truth. I had bottled my emotions up and tried to show my happy face, but all it had done was delay the inevitable. Michelle had worked out exactly what I had been doing.

Summary

After the euphoria of my first session with Michelle had worn off, I wondered if I had actually taken a massive step backwards. All of a sudden, everything that was wrong in my life was laid out in front of me. It made for sad and rather terrifying viewing.

As I wondered if coaching was really right for me, I knew deep down that things had to change, but it would take a fraught second session with Michelle for me to accept this.

This was a low point in my life. Can we take any lessons from it? Of course we can:

- Stay in the moment, especially when you're in the company of people you care about. Instead of wasting time anticipating what they may or may not say, really listen and understand what they mean. Check back with them to make sure you are on the same wavelength – Michelle would often repeat my words back to me so that I knew she had listened and understood.

- Focus on positives. When you focus on negatives, your life naturally goes in a negative direction. The same is true for positives. You will achieve far more by being positive and the negatives will start to disappear.

- Block the mind chatter and distractions and focus on what you can control. Working on what you can't control is a waste of time and energy. Dealing with the things you have control over will propel your life to greater things.

- Only you can make the changes you need in your life. If you don't change, things will stay exactly as they are. Is that really what you want? It's no one else's fault if life isn't treating you the way you'd like it to treat you; it's up to you to make changes.

Michelle, as usual, was right: I had to find the courage to commit to making changes. I just didn't know how.

10
The Energy Drain

As I sat at my desk at work, the noise of the office swirled around me, tempting me to join in the chaos. I sat listlessly, believing that the business I had put my blood, sweat and tears into building had turned against me. I was sick of working to pay people's salaries and having nothing to show for it myself. The long days and often nights had taken their toll. I was shattered.

I sat, hoping someone would notice how unhappy I was. I hoped someone would step up, take over from me and sort my problems out. No one did. Not even Kate noticed how bad I was feeling.

In a moment of frustration, I got up and walked out, not looking back or telling the staff where I was going.

I couldn't – I had no idea myself where I was going or what I would do when I got there.

The walk down the winding staircase seemed a long one. I was in a daze, not noticing any of my surroundings. Then the fresh air that hit me outside woke me up. Where should I go? I desperately wanted someone to talk to, but there was no one who understood. Even Michelle didn't seem to understand what I was going through.

I walked to my Porsche and sat in the lovely red leather seat. There, in my beautiful car, a wave of emotion came over me. *I'm a fraud*, I thought. *I have a lovely house I don't live in, a lovely car I can't afford and a lifestyle that is a lie. People think I'm a success, but I can't even run my company. It runs me.*

I dreamed of starting the company over again, how I would do things differently. How the staff would respect me and work hard for me. How I would be happy and confident, a success and proud of my business. Everything was exciting and I loved the pictures in my head.

'That's what I want to do,' I said out loud. 'I'll start again. I'll sell this damn business and start a new one. Life will be exciting and I will be happy. I'll do better next time and build the business I really want.'

As I fired up the engine, pressing the accelerator and hearing the roar, I felt like something inside was roaring as well. In that moment, I really believed I had clarity. Everything was going to be OK and I couldn't wait to see Michelle to tell her.

A problem shared

'I'm selling,' I told Michelle excitedly at our next appointment. 'I've decided I've had enough. I finally have clarity.'

'What made you decide to sell?' she asked. I explained how the company had dragged me down, taken all the fun from my life. I hated it with a passion and had given up on it. I wanted to do something else.

'I can't wait for it to be sold,' I said. 'The company is no good for me.' I went on to tell Michelle how excited I was to start a new business, a better business. A business that would run itself without me. As I spoke, I felt relieved, as if I already had this new business. I talked enthusiastically about how things would be different, how happy I would be and how much money I would make.

'I've noticed a change of energy, Lee,' Michelle said. 'Tell me where this excitement is coming from.'

'It's just so good to talk to someone. I have no one I can talk to, other than you – and myself, of course,' I joked.

'What do you mean by that?' Michelle asked. I explained how I often felt alone with my problems and would constantly talk to myself to come up with the solutions.

'I run scenarios through my head constantly. I have to sort everything out myself as I'm the boss and have no one to turn to. I can't talk to my parents as they don't understand what I do. I could never talk to Debbie; she'd worry far too much. I have no choice but to talk to myself, and you.'

'What about friends? Or other businesspeople?' Michelle asked.

'No way, I'd look weak and vulnerable. You can't be seen as weak in business, Michelle, you will get taken advantage of. No one will be able to take advantage of me.'

'That's interesting, Lee,' Michelle said thoughtfully. 'Do your staff ever come to you with their problems?'

'All the bloody time,' I said. 'I'm sure I've told you that before. They never stop telling me their problems, even their personal ones, and I sort everything out for them. I feel like a social worker most days.'

'How do your staff respond when you sort their problems out for them?'

'They are grateful for my help.'

'And how do you feel when you help them?' Michelle asked.

'I feel good,' I said. 'I moan about them, but when I help them sort a problem, I like it. I like to be the one they come to.'

Michelle paused for a moment. 'So when you sort out your staff's problems, both you and they feel good. Is that what I heard?' she asked.

'Yes, that's right,' I replied.

'How do you think your staff would feel if you let them help you with your problems?'

I was about to say they would probably feel good, but I couldn't allow myself to form the words. Instead, I told Michelle it was different for me. I was the boss and couldn't share problems. If I did, I would look weak. Michelle listened as I told her how I needed to be strong to protect myself and everyone around me. I had to sort my own mess out. I talked and talked in the hope Michelle would forget to ask me more about sharing problems with others.

The chatter in my head

Michelle hadn't forgotten. 'Correct me if I'm wrong, Lee,' she said. 'Your staff may be able to help you and may enjoy helping you, but you won't talk to them as you will look weak. Is that right?'

'Yes,' I replied.

'So you talk to yourself about your problems as you have no one else to talk to.'

'All the time,' I said. 'I have hundreds of conversations with myself every day. It's got so bad I actually move my mouth when I talk to myself. I can't stop it.' My mood dampened as I spoke these words. 'I talk to myself because sometimes I need intelligent conversation,' I joked, trying to lighten the atmosphere.

Michelle let out a little laugh and admitted she was sometimes guilty of doing the same thing. Then she asked another question.

'How does it make you feel to constantly have these conversations in your head?'

I sat and wondered how honest I should be. I felt safe at Michelle's house and had confidence she wouldn't use what I said against me, so decided to tell the truth.

'I feel exhausted. I have no idea what's going on around me most days as I'm constantly trying to solve every problem in my personal or business life. They're running through my head all day. I function basically as a person, but I'm never fully functioning as my mind is always elsewhere.

'I feel lonely and out of control. I've lost all my friends. Annabelle wants to spend quality time with me, but I'm too tired. Spinning all these plates – my separation, new home and business – is crippling me.'

As we both sat in silence, I slumped down in my chair, looking at the floor and wanting it to swallow me up. My eyes became heavy and I wanted to sleep. I was exhausted again; the excitement from the start of the meeting had gone. Telling Michelle how I felt had taken everything from me. I had shown her a side that I'd hidden away for years, and I wasn't sure how I felt about it.

On the one hand, I was relieved that someone recognised my pain and wasn't judging me or going to use it against me. But I was confused about what to say next. Michelle wasn't talking and seemed to be waiting for me to add more.

'I don't know how to stop it. I want to stop the chatter in my head and have more energy to enjoy time with Annabelle and my work, but I can't do it.'

'What would happen if you could stop the voices in your head?' Michelle asked.

Ironically, I was having a conversation in my head at that very moment, talking to myself about the best way to answer the question. It made me laugh a little.

'I need to find the perfect scenario. When I work out what needs to be said and done, only then can I make sure everything works well.'

'Lee, when you have a conversation in your head and work out the perfect scenario, how often does the reality go exactly as you planned it?' Michelle asked.

'Never,' I fired back. 'It never does.' As I spoke these words, I felt slightly stupid. I realised the implication of them, but I couldn't backtrack. I also knew that if I'd answered, 'All the time,' Michelle would have known I was lying.

Checkmate, I thought. *She's got me. I have no way out of this one.*

I looked at Michelle and smiled. 'I see what you did there, you are very clever. I know the internal conversations are a waste of my time and energy, but I just can't stop them.'

'Am I right in thinking you have the conversations to make sure everything is perfect?'

'Yes,' I replied.

'Who do you know who is perfect?' Michelle asked.

I thought for a while and couldn't come up with anyone. Then I mentioned social media and the people I saw online. I explained how I regarded the image they portrayed as perfect, but also fake. As I sat and thought of perfection, I admitted to Michelle that I didn't really like perfect people that much anyway. I found them irritating. As I talked, I started to realise that striving for perfection was a waste of time.

Then Michelle asked, 'If you didn't have endless internal conversations and constantly strive for perfection, how would you feel?'

'Relieved,' I answered. 'And I'd have more energy.'

'How do you think you having more energy would impact on your relationship with Annabelle?'

'It would be great if I had more energy. I'd have more fun with her and I'd appreciate her more.'

This was all I needed to say. The thought of having more energy for Annabelle was so exciting. However, as quickly as the excitement rose, it came crashing down.

'Wait,' I said in frustration, 'I have no idea how to change. I don't think I'm capable of not chatting to myself.'

Michelle then asked what it was about perfection that annoyed me.

'It's not real,' I told her. 'Nothing is perfect, it can always be improved. When things aren't perfect, they're more real and actually better, as they can be worked on.'

'Are you saying that imperfect is better than perfect?' Michelle asked.

'I think so,' I replied. 'Yes, I am saying that.'

'When you catch yourself talking to yourself, could you tell the voice in your head it's OK not to be perfect and he can shut up for now?'

'I could try it. I think that could work.'

'Lee,' Michelle said, 'you may not notice every time you talk to yourself to begin with, but that's OK. Get into the habit of noticing and you will get better at it. Then you can tell the voice to stop.'

'That's fine, Michelle, I don't have to be perfect,' I joked. We both laughed as the session came to an end.

As I walked away, I felt good. For the first time in who knows how long, I didn't feel the need to be perfect. I understood nothing is ever perfect and I could let go a bit. And if I could stop wasting my time with stupid conversations in my head, I would have more energy for life. Things would get better.

Then I realised I was talking to myself about how life would improve if I would just stop talking to myself, and I told myself to shut up.

Summary

I had a lot to tell Michelle at our third session together, but the meeting didn't end as I had expected. From stating that I hated my business and wanted nothing more than to sell it, I left realising it was the endless chatter in my head – the chatter I had believed was essential to work through my problems – that was actually draining me of energy.

What could I do to stop the internal chatter? And were there other ways I could improve things at work, and as a result improve my whole life? Let's have a look at what I learned:

- Aiming for perfection is a waste of time. What seems perfect to others may not be to you. Do things as well as you can, and then either get help to improve them or go with what you have got. This saves time, effort and money.

- If you find yourself constantly solving other people's problems and it makes you feel good, consider how good it may make them feel to return the compliment and help you with yours.

- Trying to predict how scenarios in your life or business will turn out is fruitless as they are never likely to go the way you expected. The inner chatter this leads to is exhausting and will drain you of energy, and the scenarios may not even materialise in the end. Instead, tackle problems only when they appear, and be sure to ask for help when you need it.

- The business world is full of people who will be only too happy to guide you, so find a network of support. No one worth knowing is going to regard you as weak if you ask them for help; if they do, they are not the sort of person you want around you.

I had a new perspective on perfection and a resolve to tell my inner chatter to shut up. How would this change my life?

11
A Pivotal Meeting

'How's the head chatter?' Michelle asked at our next meeting.

'It's not too bad,' I said. 'I've caught myself having quite a few conversations and told myself to shut up. I used to lie in bed for hours, talking through situations, but I've got into the habit of telling myself that my brain would better serve me by getting a good night's sleep.'

'How does that make you feel?' asked Michelle excitedly.

'Great. I feel so much better, sleeping soundly makes a massive difference. I'm more awake the next day and have more energy to do what I want. I feel like I've made some progress.'

As I talked, I couldn't help noticing I was more open to conversation. I wasn't pushing back and felt a little more relaxed. Up to now, I had always been rigid and guarded; I had a suit of armour that Michelle hadn't fully got behind, but I was starting to feel lighter and happier.

I decided to share this with Michelle. 'I feel better,' I said. 'I know I have a long way to go, but I'm in a better place than I was.'

I went on to say that I still felt selling my business was for the best; I wanted to get out and start over but was scared to lose my income. The conflict between selling and sorting the business out confused me and I needed clarity on what to do.

'I get the fact you don't tell me what to do, but I don't get how talking to you makes me feel so much better,' I said.

'Why do you think it makes you feel better?' Michelle asked.

'I guess it's because I get things off my chest. I don't have to bottle everything up and I can be myself here.'

To change or not to change?

Michelle wanted to know more about me 'being myself', so I went on to explain.

'In the "real" world, I have to keep everything bottled up. I don't let my hair down; I work all the time. To me, protecting my business means making sure no one sees my problems. I cover everything up and put on a brave face to show everything is OK, even when it's not. When I want something, I don't tell anyone. That way, they can't steal my ideas.

'It used to be easy because I could be Lee the businessman at work, then myself at home. But the more problems I had, the more time I spent worrying. Then I had to hide my real self from Debbie too, so I stayed Lee the businessman all the time. Talking to you, Michelle, I can be myself for the first time in years.'

'We talked last time about trusting people and opening up to them, asking if they could help you sort your problems. You said you couldn't do that as you needed to protect others and your business. Is that still true?'

'Yes, it is.'

'If you could talk to everyone as you do with me, what impact may that have on your life?' Michelle asked.

'Oh, that would be wonderful. I would be so happy and I'd get everything off my chest.' But as I spoke about how great it would be to talk to others, a dark cloud gathered over me and swallowed my energy. I slumped down in the chair and muttered the words, 'I can't do that.'

'I've noticed a real change in energy,' Michelle said quietly. 'Tell me what you are thinking.'

I felt like I'd lost the winning lottery ticket at that precise moment. The hope of gaining clarity was gone; I was alone and worried again.

'I have no one,' I said. 'Friends have stopped phoning as I always said no to going out, and I've lost Debbie too. My parents are lovely, but don't understand business; my staff mustn't know anything about my problems; and I'd look a right idiot talking to random strangers. I feel trapped.'

'Tell me more about being trapped, Lee.'

'I have nowhere to go, no one to talk to. I do everything alone and can't get out. Selling the business is my only way to escape, but if I sell, I will lose my income and may make all the same mistakes with the next business. So I don't sell and feel more and more trapped. It's a vicious circle.

'I do feel better now I don't have so many stupid conversations in my head, but I still have nowhere to go.'

I felt the life drain from my body as I lapsed into silence, pondering on just how bad things had got. Nothing seemed to work anymore, fun was long gone from my life. My only enjoyment was time with Annabelle, but even that relationship was in trouble.

A wave of emotion overcame me. I could see how I had pushed everyone away, knew why people had stopped talking to me and trusting me.

'I'm the problem,' I said, fighting back the tears.

'Why do you say that?' Michelle asked softly.

'I don't share problems. My aim is to appear strong, but instead I confuse people. Debbie lived with someone she didn't understand, my friends gave up on me because I wouldn't ask for help and my staff are confused because I keep my plans in my head. I only tell them bits of what is going on to protect myself in case things go wrong.'

'How does it feel to say those words, Lee?' Michelle's voice was still quiet.

'I don't know. Kind of good, but sad. I feel a bit of an idiot, but also proud that I have done so much on my own. It's weird: I don't really know how to feel.'

'That's really interesting, Lee. Tell me more.'

I let out a big sigh and thought for a while. 'I've built so much on my own. I dragged that company out of the gutter and turned it around, despite having no care knowledge. I was a mortgage broker who re-invented himself and I had to learn fast. It took so much of my time, effort and energy, almost everything I had, but I kept going and never gave up.

'I did all this by making decisions myself and trusting no one. I feel proud of that, but also stupid. If I had got help, I may have taken the company higher and had way fewer problems. Does that make sense?'

'Absolutely,' Michelle said. 'What do you think you could have done differently to make things better?'

'I don't know,' was my quick-fire reply. The energy was returning to my body and I had perked up a bit. 'I've been like this for so long, I'm not sure I can change. I don't know if I want to change. I've got myself this far, so maybe life isn't that bad after all.'

Michelle waited, I guess to make sure I'd finished talking. Then she said, 'I asked you what you would do differently to make things better and you talked about changing. Why do you think you said that?'

As I thought, a little smile came over my face. Bloody hell, she was good. Checkmate – she had got me again.

'I guess to do things better, I need to change,' I said as I looked Michelle squarely in the eye. 'I know what you are getting at. You want me to talk to people about my problems, you want me to ask for help, but I can't see that happening. What if they steal my ideas? What if they think I'm weak and take advantage?'

'What if they don't?' Michelle asked.

Michelle's story

As I sat confused, Michelle told me a story.

'When I was younger, I wanted to get out of the city life. It was draining me and I was tired of it. Every day was a problem. I hated the train ride, the office, the people, everything. All I talked about was problems.

'After a month of listening to me ranting about all the bad stuff, my husband asked me what was good in my life. In that moment, I could not think of one single thing. I had become so used to focusing on what was bad, I only looked for bad things. I never saw the good in anything or anyone.

'It was my husband who taught me that we get what we focus on. After I started focusing on the good, things turned around. Good things happened to me, life got better and I enjoyed myself again. That is why I work on getting my clients to find clarity. When they have complete clarity on what they want to do, they focus on getting it.'

I was taken aback. Michelle had gone through a similar situation to mine. She always seemed so relaxed and confident; I would never have guessed she had problems like everyone else.

I sat and thought as Michelle's story sank in, then said, 'If people don't steal my ideas and take advantage of me, then they may help.'

'Tell me more,' Michelle said.

'If they don't think I'm weak, they may help me sort problems instead of adding to them.'

Michelle reminded me that I had told her in the last session how good I felt when I helped others.

'Is there a possibility that others may have the same feeling if they help you?' she asked. It was similar to a question she had asked in our last session, but this time, I found the words to respond.

'I guess so. I don't know until I try, but I'm not sure if I want to.'

'And that's OK,' said Michelle. 'You may decide you don't want to change and will carry on as you are. Whatever you choose is your prerogative, but tell me something, Lee. If you do ask for help and open up to people, how could that benefit you?'

'It could be good. I may get help and people may understand what pressure I'm under and offer to do more. I could then start enjoying life again.'

'Hmmm, that's interesting. You may get help and people may do more for you, which would lead to you enjoying life. Is that right?'

'Yes, that's right,' I replied.

My biggest weakness

Michelle then switched the conversation from work. 'Tell me, how do you think Annabelle feels when you don't open up to her?'

On hearing that question, I felt the need to defend myself. I didn't want to start talking about Annabelle's feelings, so explained to Michelle that Annabelle was a child and didn't understand. She was OK as long as I played with her.

Michelle wasn't about to give up that easily. 'I get that, Lee, but kids are often more observant than we give them credit for. When Annabelle sees you stressed and worried or notices you talking to yourself, what do you think she feels?'

'You will have to ask her,' I snapped. The thought of my behaviour affecting Annabelle negatively was playing on my mind. I'd assumed I had done a great job of hiding my multitude of problems to protect her, but now wasn't so sure. Since the separation, Annabelle had had her troubles like any kid would, but I still considered I'd done a good job of looking after her. It agitated me that Michelle seemed to be questioning my ability to care for my daughter.

'I sense a little anger,' Michelle stated.

'I do my best every day! Life is hard: I am dealing with a separation, the business is in trouble, and now you dare question how I make my Annabelle feel?' I was ranting, but couldn't stop myself.

'Maybe I didn't word my question well,' Michelle said. 'What I mean is, if Annabelle were to understand how you feel, do you think she would benefit in any way?'

'I don't think so,' I insisted. 'She is a child and wouldn't understand. I can't tell her because I need to protect her. She is the only good thing I've got left; I can't upset her any more than I have already.'

'Let's say, Lee, you were able to take off your armour and talk openly and honestly to everyone. Let's say the happy Lee came back to life – how would that affect your relationship with Annabelle?'

I couldn't help smiling at that. Michelle clearly knew Annabelle was my weakness, the one person I would do anything for, and I thought I realised the direction she was taking the conversation. I had to second guess her to protect myself.

'My armour is ingrained in me, I can't take it off,' I said. 'I need to be strong so I can protect Annabelle. I need my armour to show everyone I'm the boss and in control.'

'You said earlier that you feel good helping people. Is that still true?'

'Yes,' I said warily.

'You also said people may be able to help, if you'd open up to them. Is that still true?'

'I think I said that. OK, yes.'

'Lee, how can you expect people to feel good about helping you and know how to help you if you cover yourself in this protective armour?' Michelle asked.

I sat thoughtfully, wondering how I could get myself out of this one. Things were becoming uncomfortable, and I didn't like it.

'If I take my armour off, I'm kind of vulnerable. I can be attacked. People may take advantage, or they may not. It's a gamble I'm not sure I want to take.'

'Let's say you gamble and it goes really well for you. How do things look in your life then?' asked Michelle.

'Great. Everyone helps and takes work away from me. I have more time and freedom. My business runs well without me and I have energy for Annabelle. I can make her happy and go on holidays with her. It would be awesome.'

'Time with Annabelle, energy for Annabelle and holidays with Annabelle,' Michelle repeated. 'How does that sound?'

'Brilliant,' I said. 'Absolutely brilliant.'

'What if you gamble and it goes badly? What's the worst thing that can happen?' Michelle asked.

In the excitement of imagining a holiday with Annabelle, I forgot about my armour and replied, 'Not much, really. Life would go on. I'd be doing the same old stuff I'm used to doing. I can deal with that, been doing it for years.'

'Would you say, in the light of what you've just told me, that taking off your armour and being vulnerable could be a positive?'

'Oh yes,' I said without thinking, 'most definitely. People would see the real me and I think they'd like what they see. I'm actually a fun person who enjoys a laugh. If they got to know that side of me, they may be more inclined to help me.'

'How does it feel when you say those words?'

I looked up at Michelle and said sadly, 'I'm not sure if I can.'

Michelle asked for clarification.

'People see me in a certain way. I like who I have become because I get respect as the boss. People look up to me and it feels good. Although my life is hard, I still have way more than most. I should be grateful and happy.'

As I said these words, I felt defeated. The thought of opening myself up to others was exciting, while the thought of not being able to was scary. That would mean I had settled for how things were.

'What are you thinking?' Michelle asked.

'That maybe I should give it a go and see what happens. Maybe it would benefit me. I mean, what have I got to lose? Things can't get any worse.'

'How do you think you could, as you say, "give it a go"?' asked Michelle.

I thought for a while. 'I will be honest with people and let them know how I feel,' I replied. 'If someone asks me how I am, I'll tell them. I won't pretend everything is OK when it isn't. Maybe I can start there.

'I will have a meeting at work and tell the staff exactly how things are, be upfront and ask for help. Then I can see what the result is. Hopefully, they won't think badly of me.'

'What about with Annabelle?' Michelle asked.

'Don't push it,' I replied jokingly. 'One step at a time.'

Michelle agreed that I would start by being open and honest with my staff, sharing my feelings and seeking help.

'See how it goes and report back,' she advised.

Feeling nervous, I was also intrigued to see if this new approach would help. I was nervous as I was about to open up to my colleagues and try something new. To do this, I would be straying well out of my comfort zone.

If they hate me for telling them how I feel, I'll sack them all, I joked to myself as I walked through the office door to put my plan into action.

Summary

This chapter has covered a hugely pivotal moment in my life. I finally realised that I had nothing to lose by being honest and open with people, and I had everything to gain, most importantly a great relationship with my daughter. I'd have the time and energy to make sure our days together were top quality, and I would always be sharing the moment with her. The mere thought was enough to bring a huge smile to my face.

If you are struggling to open up to others, you're not alone. Even Michelle had to be honest with her husband before she saw the need to change. Change is a choice we all have, but I know only too well how daunting it can seem.

Let's have a look at the approaches that worked for me:

• Focus on the positives and you will naturally attract the life you want. Visualise what a happy life looks like for you. Is it having more free time? Playing with your kids? Going on holiday every other month? Getting fit? Driving a sports car?

Whatever it is, that's your motivation.
Concentrate on that as you make the changes you
need to achieve it.

- Be upfront and tell people how you feel.
This removes any chance of confusion and
misunderstanding. Take down your armour or
whatever you use to protect yourself. Let people
see the real you. They'll probably like that side of
you far more than falseness as most people can
spot it when you're being false. And when people
like you, they'll probably be willing to help you.

- Be aware that children are more perceptive than
we adults tend to give them credit for. In trying to
be strong for your kids, are you actually pulling
away from them and damaging your relationship
with them? If you don't have kids, maybe you are
damaging your relationship with your partner,
family or friends in this way, and that's a sad and
lonely place to be. Believe me, I know.

- If you don't like the direction your life is
going in, get out of your comfort zone and try
new approaches. It's not easy, but it will pay
dividends. Doing the same old thing will only
bring the same result.

Finally, I could see a way to improve my life. I had
found the clarity I craved, but would I have the courage to make the change?

12
I Am Enough

'It's been a week since we last met, Lee, how are things?' Michelle asked.

'I can't believe this is our last session together. They have gone so quickly.'

'Yes,' replied Michelle, 'the sessions have gone quickly and we have made some nice discoveries together. Last time, we talked about you opening up with people at work and letting yourself be vulnerable. How did that go?'

I didn't need to think about my answer, I was so excited to tell Michelle the good news.

'Oddly enough, it went well,' I said. 'I can't believe how much things have changed for me in one week.'

Everyone needs a goal

I'd had one of my best weeks for a long time. As soon as I'd returned to the office the previous Friday, before I could change my mind, I'd met with my staff and told them how I was feeling about the business. I'd even had a chat with Annabelle over the weekend, telling her how much I missed her and how sad I had become in life. Testing the water, I had been open and honest with everyone.

'People at work were shocked, but pleased,' I said. 'They all agreed to feeling the same as me about the business, but no one was sure what to do. They told me that I would make plans, but only share the bare bones with them. Then I would forget what I had said, which frustrated them so much, they pushed back and left everything for me to do, but this was only because they didn't know what to do – I'd never made it clear, so of course they were confused. Now I was being honest and open with them, they rose to the challenge and started suggesting ideas. I couldn't believe it.'

'What did you do when you heard how they had been feeling, Lee?' Michelle asked.

'At first, I felt a bit angry. I believed they should have known what to do, but then I realised I changed what they were meant to be doing so many times, it was no wonder they were confused. So I apologised and asked them what they wanted to do.

'It was amazing: they asked if they could do more, not less. It frustrated them when I took over their projects or sorted problems they could deal with themselves. They didn't like the work simply because they felt restricted and never got the satisfaction of completing anything.'

'Can you imagine playing football and not having any goals to shoot for?' Michelle asked. 'Or playing golf with no holes to putt?'

'That would be boring,' I said. 'I get it: everyone needs something to aim for in life, otherwise we'll never be satisfied.

'I've agreed to do something new with the staff. They know their jobs well, so I am going to trust them to do the work. I've agreed that when they do well, I will praise and reward them, and when they don't, I will help them understand why so they can improve. They know now that if they all do well, the company will grow and we will all be rewarded. If they keep failing and not learning from their mistakes, then I will need to make uncomfortable changes. They understand and are happy with that.'

'How do you feel?' asked Michelle.

'I feel good, but nervous. In some ways I feel like a failure, but I don't know why.'

'That's interesting, Lee. If you are OK with it, I'd like to explore that more, but first, tell me about Annabelle.'

Father and daughter

I felt my face light up as I spoke. 'I told Annabelle how I was feeling, how sad I was and how many problems I had at work. I told her I was getting help to change and I was sorry if I'd pushed her away. I got everything out in the open and it felt good.

'At first, Annabelle told me it was OK, that I was the best daddy in the world and I didn't need to change. Then she asked if I could put my phone away when I'm with her. She said she thought I cared more about work than her.

'When she said that, my world changed, Michelle. I realised just how distracted I had become. My life was a constant round of sorting out other people's problems and I never focused on what is important.

'I've changed that now. My staff are doing great. They are not nervous about failing, as they can learn from their mistakes, and they know what to aim for. They don't bother me as much, except to tell me when they have succeeded because they want that reward. It's great when they come to me with good news. I feel amazing.

'As a result, I don't get distracted by work as much now. When I am with Annabelle, the phone goes away and she loves it. I give her my full attention. Our relationship has improved just by me focusing only on her. I feel free. It's great.'

I was smiling and happy for the first time in years as I reflected on my achievement. All it had taken was open and honest conversations to show how I was feeling and allow people to see a vulnerable side to me.

Michelle, though, brought the mood down slightly when she returned to my comment about still feeling like a failure.

From a fraud to a success

'I never finish or achieve anything,' I said. 'I know I have done well. I earned a lot of money in mortgages, drive a Porsche, and pay for the big house Debbie lives in and the rent on my flat. I've built a business that now has a million-pound turnover and things are better than ever. But I feel like a fraud, like I start something, get halfway through, and then move on to something else without completing the first task.'

'What happens to whatever you were doing when you leave it to move on to something else?' Michelle asked.

'I either give up on it because it wasn't working or let someone else take over. But it's frustrating, never finishing anything.'

'What would it mean to you to start and finish something?'

'That would be great,' I said. 'If I could do something from start to finish, that would be amazing. I don't think I have ever finished anything in my whole life; I always get distracted or give up.

'Take a business for example. I love setting it up, putting all the pieces together and getting started, but as soon as it gets to the day-to-day grind, I lose interest. I don't like that side of it; I then want to leave and do something else. It annoys me, though. I should be grateful and happy with what I have got. Instead, I am sad and down because I feel trapped. Nothing ever seems to satisfy me.

'Even now, although I'm happy about the staff doing well and I have more time and energy, I still want to walk away and start something new. I want the excitement of planning and building to come back. I have less to do now, which I thought was what I wanted, but it's not really. Now I want to do more. It's confusing.'

'You talked about how you should be grateful. Tell me more about that,' said Michelle.

'I have more than most people, but I always want even more. I don't ever seem to be satisfied or happy. I pick up and drop projects, never getting anywhere. Or at least, that is how it feels.'

Michelle sat and thought for a while. 'If you got somewhere, how would you know when you'd arrived?' she asked.

As I sat and pondered on my answer, I became confused about where 'somewhere' was. What was I aiming for? My staff seemed to know where they were going and be happy, but what about me? I'd thought I wanted to sell my business a couple of weeks ago, but now I wasn't so sure. Maybe keeping it would be better for me.

'I have no idea,' I said. 'If the business runs well without me, maybe I should keep it. I have so many ideas all the time, it's hard to know where I'm going.' As I said these words, I felt myself sinking and becoming overwhelmed. My bright mood at the start of the session was gone, replaced with uncertainty.

'You came here wanting clarity, Lee. What does clarity mean to you?' Michelle asked.

'Knowing where I'm going would give me clarity.'

'Would knowing where you're going stop you feeling like a fraud and unsatisfied?'

'It would stop me feeling unsatisfied because I'd know when I had achieved things. I'm not sure about feeling like a fraud. I've always felt this way. I think I'm lucky to have got to where I am, but I never finish anything and things are a mess. Then I get frustrated and feel like even more of a fraud.'

'That's interesting, Lee. What does not finishing mean to you?'

'What do you think it means?' I fired back.

'I don't know, Lee. I have no idea what not finishing something means to you. Only you can tell me that.'

'It frustrates the hell out of me. I let everyone down and people get fed up with me. I can't see anything through to the end because there is so much to do.' I then went off into a rant about how busy I was and how many people needed me. I told Michelle yet again about how demanding my business was and how I had to juggle so much.

'Lee,' Michelle said thoughtfully, 'can you think of a successful person who has lots of businesses and projects on the go?'

I didn't need to think. 'Richard Branson,' I replied. 'He is always doing things. That man starts loads of businesses and owns so much. I have no idea how he does it.'

'Do you think he sees everything through from start to end?' Michelle asked.

'No way,' I said, getting excited. 'He has ideas and creates things, then he gives the ideas to others to complete. I suppose he keeps himself informed on progress, but he trusts other people to take his ideas and run with them.'

'So what you are saying is one of the most successful businesspeople on the planet has ideas, starts them and gives them to others to complete. Then he goes on to create more ideas and opportunities for others, but he never completes the task himself. Does that remind you of anyone, Lee?'

That statement hit me like a hammer to my stomach. It had an immediate effect. In an instant, my perspective changed. I started thinking about myself as a success, not a fraud.

'If it's good enough for Branson, then it's good enough for me,' I said quietly as I considered the comparison.

'What do you mean?' asked Michelle.

'He doesn't finish every project he creates. He has ideas and takes them as far as he wants, then hands them over to someone else to do the rest. He gets more done that way, can keep creating and moving forward. I kind of do that but get frustrated and sometimes forget to find people to pass the idea on to, so it gets lost.'

Playing to my strengths

I was getting emotional. For years, I had thought I wasn't good enough, a quitter and an underachiever. I had led a life of frustration, self-doubt and negativity. The depression I had suffered around my failing business was because I hadn't realised how far to take things before I got help. I had created so much, but I hadn't reached my potential because I never shared my creations with the people around me. I had never engaged with them correctly. Instead of getting them to help me, I tried to do everything myself. It was a one-way street that constantly caused me to lose focus and get distracted.

Now, as the tears entered my eyes, I realised Michelle had just compared me to Sir Richard Branson. I could see the similarity – we had a common trait. For as long as I could remember, I had been told I wasn't good enough. Now, I had the potential to emulate one of the most successful people in business.

'For some people, starting a project then passing it on to others is their talent,' said Michelle enthusiastically. 'Maybe that is your talent, Lee.'

'I've always seen it as a failure,' I said. 'But instead of fussing and fussing to get things right, then giving up, I should have found people who are better suited than me to seeing a project through and let them complete it. I would have achieved so much more.

'It would be awesome to work in this way. Maybe I could be as rich as Richard Branson.'

'What do you want to do from now on?' Michelle asked.

'Michelle, I think I have clarity. I finally understand myself. I have ideas and I have passion to start them, but I don't have the ability or desire to see them through to the end on my own. I need help with that, and now I'm OK with that knowledge. I've realised that I can't do everything myself. If I want a business that gives me freedom and wealth, I need people to help me.

'From now on, I will create my ideas and find people to complete them for me. I will not feel a failure when I don't finish something myself; I will feel empowered.'

Michelle looked at me, the big smile on her face indicating she knew her job was done.

'Lee, for the first time since we met, I feel like I am seeing the real you. When you first came, you wanted me to give you the answers. You were closed and frustrated, and you kept everything to yourself. You wanted complete control and were scared to be vulnerable in front of others.

'Now you speak openly about your feelings and seek help. You have recognised that what you do is enough, and when you are ready to hand something over to someone else, that means you have completed that task. How does that feel?'

I sat quietly; I couldn't talk through the wave of emotion I was feeling. A massive weight had been removed from my stomach and I felt lighter in my body and mind. For years, I had tried to prove to everyone I was the man who could go the distance. No matter how many hits I took, I could always get back up and go again. I'd felt so much pain as my business kicked and punched me over the years, but I knew no other way. Now, all of a sudden, I could see another way.

As I let that sink in, I finally replied. 'Knowing that I am enough and I do enough means so much to me. I thought I was a failure because I gave up on projects. Then I would start something new to justify giving up on what I had previously been working on. I've tried to keep going for far too long and have burned myself out. It was a vicious circle that got me down. Now, I've learned that asking for help is a good thing, and that's massive for me.

'I feel great, knowing that I can start as many projects as I want and ask others to complete them for me. Doing enough and being happy with what I'm doing will lead to less distractions. I will have more energy and will be free to spend time with my daughter and enjoy it. I can take time off while others work on my ideas. It will be hard for me to change everything straight away, but I can do it. Your sessions have given me a whole new way of thinking and working.'

'Do you need to change everything straight away?' Michelle asked.

'Not really,' I replied. 'I've got this far as the old me, so making some small changes to start with will be OK.'

'That's sensible,' Michelle said. 'When we make little changes and build them into our routine, it's easier to adapt to them. All you need to do is commit to making a small change every day. Some days will be good and some not so good, so tell me, Lee, what will you do on the not-so-good days?'

My first reaction was to say, 'Try harder and try again', but I paused and thought.

'I'll ask for help, Michelle,' I replied. 'I may even come back and sit in this chair to talk to you.'

As I left Michelle for the last time, I looked up to the sky and let out a deep breath. 'I'm enough,' I said to myself. 'With the right help, I can achieve anything.'

Summary

I hadn't understood up to now how being vulnerable and asking for help could change my life. I also hadn't realised that knowing when to hand tasks over to others was the clarity I needed. Now all of a sudden, it made sense. Richard Branson, a successful leader with a lot of energy and drive, was renowned for having ideas then handing them over to people better able to see them through. When Michelle compared me to him, I could see the traits we had in common.

Are there things that make you unhappy in your life, things that make you feel like a fraud or a failure? Here are a few hints to help you find the clarity you need, just as I did:

- To succeed in life, we can't do everything ourselves; we need the help of others. Success means having the right people around you, people who are good at the things you find difficult. Take the time to find these people.

- When you have an idea, work out how far to take it before you pass it on to someone else. This is life changing. It may be that your strength is seeing every project through to the end, but it's likely there will be some you want to give up on. Instead of dropping an idea, share it with others and explore whether the people around you can complete it instead.

- Knowing your goal will clarify when you have reached your target. And when you've reached your target, it will set you free.

13
A Bright Future

As I said goodbye to my clients, I sat back in my chair to make some notes. I wrote about the amazing transformation they had achieved and how I'd enjoyed watching them grow as a couple.

Since my coaching sessions with Michelle, I'd taken ownership of two more successful small businesses, one of which was a coaching company. Now older and wiser, I was able to reflect and enjoy the moment. I completed my notes and looked up at the beautiful surroundings of the restaurant I was sitting in. I loved to take coaching clients there on their last session to celebrate their success.

Over the years, I had taken my businesses to another level with the help of a secret: serve way more than my customers would ever expect. The restaurant meal was a surprise for clients that would wow them and make them feel special. I always booked the same table in a secluded part where it was easy and comfortable to talk while eating. The clients loved this extra touch, which also served me well in building great relationships with the people I worked with.

The last session for every client was always a celebration as I was happy they'd got the results they needed, and this time was no different from any other. The coaching had gone well, the clients had left feeling great about themselves. As usual, I lingered after they'd gone to reflect on what I had done well and what I could improve on. It was a ritual that I had come to love, but today was going to be slightly different.

A blast from the past

As I sat deep in thought, I blocked out everything going on around me. The beautiful décor of the room faded, as did the noise of diners enjoying their meals. As thoughts of my coaching session with my most recent clients ran through my head, I became conscious that someone was standing in front of me.

'Hello, Lee,' said Michelle with a twinkle in her eye. 'It's great to see you.' She looked as glamorous as ever and not a day older.

'Wow, what are you doing here?' I asked.

'I came to eat, Lee. It's a restaurant, so what do you think I'm doing here?' We both laughed as she explained she liked to visit the restaurant once a week with her friends for what she called her 'girly wine time'.

'Of course,' she said with a smile, 'wine could also mean whine time.'

'Fancy another wine?' I asked. 'The alcoholic type, I mean. It's been ages, so let's have a little drink and catch-up.'

'They will think I have pulled a toy boy, Lee,' Michelle replied, glancing over to a group of women who were looking at us and giggling. 'They are the friends I was eating with, so let me go and tell them I'm staying. They can think what they want, it will be good for my ego.'

As I ordered two dry white wines, I watched Michelle laugh and joke with her friends. They were obviously teasing her, and she was loving it. *So much energy and passion*, I told myself, thinking of how Michelle reminded me of the special person I now had in my life.

My happy life

Michelle returned and sat at my table, sipping her wine and looking me right in the eye.

'So, Lee, tell me what you want to talk about today,' she said, smiling knowingly.

'I want to thank you,' I said. 'You made everything different. When I met you, I was a mess. I was depressed and lonely; now I have a beautiful new girlfriend, my relationship with Annabelle is stronger than ever, I am a good stepfather to my partner's daughter and a dad to another little girl.'

'Lee, you are surrounded by women, so no wonder your life is great,' Michelle teased. 'Tell me more.'

'I met Aga through work, and she is beautiful. I was just thinking how much you remind me of her. She has your effervescent nature and lust for life, and that is captivating. She is also intelligent, and we talk about anything and everything. We are engaged to be married and she is my business partner as well.'

'Congratulations, she sounds amazing. And do you know what else is amazing?' Michelle asked.

'What?'

'You are,' she replied. 'You have changed so much since I first met you. In our first session, all you talked about was work and problems; now you don't mention work other than to tell me you have a business partner. Instead, you talk about your family and how great things are. You look confident and happy. Tell me, Lee, what is your secret?'

'Coaching is my secret. But you know that, don't you? Aga and I coach each other all the time, and we coach other people. It's the greatest job in the world; we both love what we do and are good at it.

'Since I met you, I've turned my life around. I used to be stressed all the time and didn't have a clue what to do. My life was going downhill fast, and I was out of control. You helped me gain the clarity I needed to make changes. The care business now works well without me; I rarely do anything there these days. I also own a gym and a coaching business. The gym runs without me as well, so I have loads of time to work in coaching as that's what I enjoy.'

'How did you get the businesses to run without you?' Michelle asked.

'You made me realise something really powerful. During our last session, I realised I was enough. Knowing this freed me to do more.'

'Aga is a doer and I'm an ideas person. We complement each other perfectly. I get a project to a certain level, and then either I outsource it or Aga takes over and completes it. We have a team around us who help us so much. Both the care and gym businesses have great managers who want to be successes. They work closely with Aga and she coaches them when they need it. Between them, the managers and Aga come up with solutions. I never hear of a problem; I only hear of solutions now.

'It's been life changing for me, working this way. It gives me free time to create ideas and test them, doing the things I'm good at and enjoy, taking the ideas as far as I want, and then passing them on to Aga or someone else if she is too busy. This simple way of working is invaluable in our personal and business lives.'

'Three businesses, three kids and a wedding to plan? Life can't always be easy – how do you cope when life gets tough?' Michelle asked.

'My life is terrible, I am surrounded by females,' I joked. 'Even our dog is a bitch. But seriously, life isn't always easy, you know that. Aga and I have our ups and downs like any couple. We nearly split at the start of our relationship, but we worked out how to deal with what life throws at us.'

I went on to explain the pressure Aga and I had been under when we got together. She had escaped an abusive relationship and I had not dated anyone in years, let alone lived with someone. It was also daunting taking on a stepchild. While things were exciting and fun at the start of our relationship, we'd made a quick decision to live together, and at first we were happy. But then things started to go wrong.

Working through our problems together

'We are compatible,' I assured Michelle, 'but we're different in many ways and this caused problems. Aga is from a small village in Poland and has views on life and traditions that are quite unlike mine. Although she is full of energy and fun, she had some limiting beliefs due to how she was treated by her ex-partner. It was confusing to live with someone from a different country who felt badly about herself. I could see so much potential in her and our life together, but got frustrated when her beliefs and way of living were out of sync with mine. I was ready for a new relationship when I fell for Aga, but until we worked each other out, there was always friction bubbling. Life with her was fun, but volatile.'

Thinking back, I found it quite funny. Aga and I were no different from any other couple getting together. We were attracted to each other, we fell in love, but we still had to learn how to understand each other. We frustrated the hell out of each other at first.

'I would try to boost her confidence, and I started to feel low again when I couldn't,' I explained to Michelle. 'Living with someone who has been abused is a challenge. I struggled and dealt with it in completely the wrong way. Some of the arguments we had were intense, to say the least. Then guess what happened?'

'You got help,' Michelle replied.

'In a way,' I said. 'I told her about my sessions with you and we started to coach each other. We read everything we could to learn about coaching, then practised on each other every day until we became so good at it, we made huge discoveries about ourselves. Just like the discovery I had with you that changed my life, when I realised that what I had thought made me a fraud was actually a trait I share with Sir Richard Branson. Aga and I changed each other's lives together.'

Michelle was on the edge of her seat. Leaning towards me, she looked excited to know more.

'We learned something amazing, and when we discovered it, it made complete sense. In the past, I would see Aga struggle, she would become down and unhappy, and this would affect me badly. It would bring me down because I often felt it was my fault, so I dealt with her unhappiness by leaving her alone to work through the problem. I would go to the gym or for a run; I thought space was what she needed. I thought that because being left alone was what I needed when I had problems. I like to have a little time to figure out how I'm feeling.

'When Aga saw me sad, on the other hand, she would smother me with questions and push and push me for an answer. It frustrated me so much as I desperately wanted the space I gave to her. It nearly tore us apart.

'Then we realised through our coaching that we were projecting our own needs on to each other. I learned that Aga needs lots of attention and conversation when she's down, otherwise she doesn't feel loved. In the past, when I left her alone, she felt betrayed, and when she smothered me with questions, I felt choked.

'Now we know what the other really needs, we give each other so much more. Just working that out brought our relationship to a whole new level. We get along so well now that when there are problems, we know exactly how we each need to deal with them. We've learned to communicate deeply, and it's been a game changer. In fact, we base a lot of our coaching sessions with clients around this type of communication.

'You did such a wonderful job with me, Michelle. You inspired me to become a coach, and I've inspired Aga to do the same. Now I coach businessmen to identify what they want in life and to become the men they and their families deserve. Jointly, Aga and I coach couples who live and work together. We know the challenges and problems these couples face, so we can help them overcome these challenges and take their home and business lives to a higher level.'

'Lee, you have what is called a niche,' Michelle said. 'You specialise in an area and it sounds like you're doing well.'

'Aga and I do well together. We don't coach from books, we coach from our own lives, our experiences and our stories. We have been through so much heartache and trouble between us, we have had such an amazing journey in life, we can easily empathise and put ourselves in our clients' shoes.

'Michelle, I remember your story about feeling trapped when you were working in London and how you changed. You empathised with what I was going through and helped me change. Aga and I do the same as you did for me, but with businessmen who are under pressure, like I was, and couples who want to go from stress to success.'

'Stress to success? I like that, Lee; I may have to steal it.'

'Stress to success is our company mission and purpose. It's why the company exists; it's what Aga and I live for. When we take people from a messy and stressful situation and help them gain clarity, everything becomes great again in their lives. They feel free and happy, they fall in love with each other all over again. Their incomes improve, everything becomes wonderful. It's amazing for us to witness. I love it and can't wait for every day to start.'

Michelle and I walked from the restaurant to our cars, two coaches happy to have met again. Michelle was pleased life had worked out well for me and she had played a part in that. I was pleased that I had been able to take what I had learned and, with Aga, create a whole new business that would help so many couples through the tough times that had devastated my relationship with Debbie all those years ago.

Summary

Aga and I are living proof that you can have a great life, a great business and do everything together as a couple. We know that our coaching works because it works for us.

There is a saying, 'When the student is ready, the teacher will appear', and I believe this to be true. I found Michelle when I was ready, people find Aga and me when they are ready to commit to the process, and we love it that way. When you commit to change, you are guaranteed to get amazing results.

Conclusion

My aim in telling my story is to show you that it is possible to go through stress, depression and heartache to become a success. In this story, I have focused on what I learned to get me through my troubles, sharing what worked for me in the hope that this will also take you from stress to success.

Business is simple; it's usually the people who confuse it. I used to confuse everything and everyone around me because I wasn't clear in what I wanted. The one thing I would like you to take from this book above all others is that it's essential to gain clarity on what you want. When you know where you're going, you can communicate this clearly and consistently.

For anything to work, you must be clear and consistent, because when everyone knows what you want and expect, life becomes easier. Don't keep everyone guessing like I did in the past when I was too scared to talk about what I wanted and what was going wrong. Don't hide away and try to deal with everything yourself until you are on the verge of breakdown.

I now have complete clarity on what I want in life and business. Of course, things go wrong. I still get down from time to time, but that's another lesson I learned: nothing is ever perfect. Before I met Michelle, I obsessed over perfection. I crippled myself because I could never let go. What a waste of time. When I realised it's OK to let go and seek help from others, my life changed for the better.

I used to look at successful and educated people and worry what others would say and think about me. During my coaching sessions, I cried with relief when I was compared to Richard Branson. All my life, I'd thought I was a failure, someone who couldn't pass an exam or get a proper job. When I realised what I do is good enough, it was life changing. Not one of us is perfect, but we are enough. When you realise this, believe me, it's liberating.

When you grow up not believing you are good enough, you naturally tend to look at successful people and wonder why what they have isn't in you. What you have is just as valuable, and you are just as capable of being a success. I no longer care what people think about me and I don't compare myself to others. Through my coaching, I know what *I* want and am capable of. I still fail, but that's OK. My wins outweigh my failures. I've learned from my mistakes and they make me appreciate my wins all the more.

I owe so much to Michelle and Aga, who have coached and supported me throughout the changes I have made in the last few years. Having the benefit of their wisdom and love has allowed me to believe in myself and made me a great coach in my own right.

When Aga and I decided to start our coaching business, it didn't go exactly as planned. We didn't get everything right first go. We chopped and changed and tweaked our message multiple times, but it was a start. In the past, I would still be tweaking the business and would probably have given up. However, I have since learned a valuable lesson.

All you have to do is jump into what you want to do. Don't wait for the perfect moment, there won't ever be one. Jump in and keep going. Then you will be unstoppable.

You are full of potential. We all have something inside that can be great. It doesn't have to be great at this stage; just a glimmer of potential is good enough to get you started. But when you recognise your potential, then you must take action. You must do something to get you going.

When Aga and I started our coaching business, we made a basic plan and got started. We told everyone we knew that we were coaches and that was it: we'd taken action. You can have all the education in the world, but if you don't commit and act, you will never get results.

Good results will fire you up as you see things moving forward. Bad results will show you that you need to tweak and change things, but that is OK. You still have the potential to succeed. Change the action you take and you will get different results.

I truly hope you have enjoyed reading this book as much as I have enjoyed writing it. I believe in what I do. I believe that given the chance, we all have the potential within to go from living in fear to becoming the men we want to be. All we need is a little help to get what's inside of us out and show it to the world.

Acknowledgements

This book so nearly never happened. In truth, what you've just read was not the book I had initially planned. My first draft was a step-by-step 'how to' business manual that was as boring as watching paint dry.

I wrote that first manuscript with good intentions – I wanted to share my vast knowledge of business – but the result was a book that offered much but was painful to read.

After months of hard work, finding the courage to rip it up and start from scratch was not an easy task.

I give so much thanks to my partner, Aga Zebrzuska, and Allan Warren for helping me realise that I could do better. I value their opinions over most, and am so happy they were open and honest with me.

The result, through their advice, is far more meaningful and accurate. Aga and Allan gave me the courage to tell my story, and for that I am so grateful.

I also give great thanks to Clare Cheeseman and Kemal Ibrahim, who spent hours checking over what I had written and advising on how I could improve it. Their feedback and support drove me to keep going and finally produce a book I am so proud to share.

Last, and not least, I offer thanks to Siam Kidd for writing my foreword. I have followed Siam for many years and worked alongside him with mastermind groups. I am honoured to have such kind words written by someone so respected within business circles.

Without these individuals' encouragement and support, this book would not be the awesome story that it is.

Thank you all.

The Author

Lee Taylor is a sought-after coach working with men who want to live without fear. He runs the Be The Man community on Facebook, where he helps busy professionals achieve work-life balance and become the men they and their families deserve.

His programme focuses on three key areas:

- Identify – work out what you really want in life

- Influence – change your thinking and environment to achieve what you want

- Income – increase income through business and investments

Lee draws on his own experiences and the lessons he's learned to help other men avoid making the same mistakes – and help them move from stress to success.

As well as running Be The Man, Lee works with his partner, Aga, to coach stressed-out couples who live and work together. Lee and Aga offer a safe and relaxed environment to help couples navigate challenges in their relationship and find ways to grow together.

Lee hosts the *Be The Man* podcast, and together, he and Aga host *The Naked Couple*, a weekly show aimed at couples who live and work together.

To connect with Lee please join his Facebook group and like his Facebook page:

f www.facebook.com/groups/647117523369598

f www.facebook.com/Coach.leetaylor

Listen to the *Be The Man* podcast on Spotify:

🟢 https://open.spotify.com/show/ 17bsT51rXmiE1ms6BC4jaX

Listen to Lee and Aga on *The Naked Couple*:

🟢 https://open.spotify.com/show/ 7ljD1lNo78wMh2Sqz2nnQc

Printed in Great Britain
by Amazon

84540517R00119